MENUHIN, Yehudi.   Violin; six lessons with Yehudi Menuhin.   Viking,
        1972 (c1971).   144p il 72-162661. 7.95.   SBN 670-74688-6

Menuhin has, in this collection of essays, put the essence of his technique at the service of the general public, and in a concise, expressive
prose style. Each of the six chapters represents a private class similar
to those which Menuhin gives at the Yehudi Menuhin School, a unique
boarding school for young musical talent which he founded in 1963
and still operates in Surrey, England. The six lessons cover breathing,
posture, positioning, stretching, bow movements and left-hand movements, and they include demonstrative diagrams. A unique contribu-
tion to the helpful literature for music educators and for music students
through college years.

YEHUDI MENUHIN is one of those rare men who have become legends in their own times. Since he has studied with three of this century's greatest musicians—Louis Persinger, Georges Enesco, and Adolph Busch—and has introduced new works either commissioned by or dedicated to him by distinguished composers all over the world, there is scarcely a great musician of the last fifty years whose path has not crossed his. His path has led him far and wide. In 1927, following great successes in Berlin, London, and New York, Mr. Menuhin initiated with his sister Hephzibah the piano-and-violin-sonata evenings which still remain highlights of concert seasons wherever they appear. Since World War II, which he spent performing extensively for men and women of the Allied Forces on both sides of the Atlantic, he has been endowed with honors of the highest order by France, Belgium, Greece, and the West German Republic. In 1965 he was made an Honorary Knight of the British Empire by Queen Elizabeth. Especially memorable among the many, many other honors he has received are the Royal Philharmonic Society's Gold Medal of 1962, the Gold Medal of the Société d'Encouragement au Progrès in 1967, the Nehru Award of 1968, and the Cobbett Medal, awarded to him by the Worshipful Company of Musicians for his services to the art of chamber music. For ten years Artistic Director of the Bath Festival (for which city, along with Edinburgh, he holds the title of Freeman), he is also Artistic Director of the annual Yehudi Menuhin Festival in Gstaad, Switzerland. He holds honorary degrees in no less than ten British Universities and is a member, patron, sponsor, or officer of nearly two hundred and fifty cultural organizations situated the world over. In recent years he has supplemented his recitals, orchestral engagements, and the conducting of chamber music and music classes by conducting three operas by Mozart. Born in New York in 1916 of Russian parents, he grew up and began his studies in San Francisco. Presently he lives in London with his wife, Diana. This is Mr. Menuhin's first book.

Yehudi Menuhin conducting a class in violin

VIOLIN

SIX LESSONS WITH
YEHUDI MENUHIN

THE VIKING PRESS · NEW YORK

Copyright © 1971 by Yehudi Menuhin

Published in 1972 by The Viking Press, Inc.
625 Madison Avenue, New York, N.Y. 10022

SBN 670-74688-6

Library of Congress catalog card number: 72-162661

Printed in U.S.A.

*To my darling Diana, without whom I should
never have known the support and peace of mind
essential to this work and – who knows the
price of sharing her husband with that other
Mistress, the Violin*

CONTENTS

PUBLISHER'S NOTE

This book grew out of six films made by James Archibald and Associates with Yehudi Menuhin, called *Violin*. The films, each of which lasts some 25 minutes, were made at the Yehudi Menuhin School of Music with a small class of children representing different stages of technical proficiency. Each film takes the form of a lesson to the class on a particular aspect of violin technique, the filming being in a documentary style so that the audience receives the benefit of a spontaneous lesson from Mr. Menuhin. The chapters of this book correspond to the six lessons on film, and amplify and explain the subject matter of each with additional exercises and illustrative diagrams.

Any enquiries for the purchase or hire of the films should be made to the Argo Record Company, 115 Fulham Road, London S.W.3., England.

ACKNOWLEDGEMENTS

The following six chapters on the basic principles of violin playing owe much of their inspiration and evolution to my School, established in 1963. It is there that in the last few years the reciprocal experience and privilege of learning and teaching has become a way of life to me.

Obviously I cannot list everyone – children and staff, as well as the myriad sources beyond – all of whom have contributed to my convictions and attitudes; but in connection with this published method, I must acknowledge my debt and express my gratitude to Peter and Margaret Norris. To Peter I am indebted for his help with the early chapters. Margaret, herself scarcely older than our older children and an excellent violinist, with wholehearted dedication and meticulous application and patience, pencil in hand when I was teaching, bow in hand when she was demonstrating, accumulated and continually tested in her supervision of the violinists our growing body of knowledge and experience.

I am grateful to my good colleague, Roger Raphael, for taking great pains in reading the manuscript and for making invaluable suggestions. He has also kindly provided descriptions for some of the exercises in Lessons II and IV.

A final word of gratitude to the man whom I sometimes call 'my best violin teacher', Mr. B. K. S. Iyengar, my yoga *guru*. Of course he is not a violinist, but some of the principles I have evolved are based on yoga and on his teaching of yoga and several of the exercises in the first lesson are his inspiration.

YEHUDI MENUHIN

INTRODUCTION

To whomever this may concern, be he teacher or beginner, advanced student or performer, I would like to address these few words about an instrument which I have known intimately for nearly fifty years, an instrument which must surely be one of the most beautiful artefacts ever created by man and one of the most capricious to handle. It is perhaps this very elusiveness that adds to its magic, for unless one is willing to become its slave, to resign oneself voluntarily and with all one's heart, the violin will take its revenge, withhold its manifold voices, withdraw its infinite range of subtleties, and you will be left holding a lovely piece of musical furniture, offended and inert.

No one violin is like another; each is as separate and particular as a human being and as differing in its response to the bow which touches its strings as a variety of people would be to one opinion.

It is in the conquering of its moods and endless modulations, in the manipulation of its voices from the most delicate of whispers to a hearty bellow that the whole vocation of violin playing lies. For the player is an independent being: no alien hand has set an arbitrary pitch, no ear but his own will dictate the tuning. He alone is master and servant, and as soon as his bow touches the instrument the marvellous battle has begun, the challenge and the response are joined and the achievement is wholly his.

It is this wonderful relationship between the violin and its player that makes it and its other stringed relations unique, and it is with the understanding of this quality that the violinist should approach his task. In this way he can never be bored, even though he may despair; never feel imposed upon, even though like the captain of a ship he will learn the infinity of horizons and know the patience and endurance this recognition exacts. The violin is indeed the very foundation of our musical culture without which none of our chamber music ensembles or symphonic repertoire could exist.

The violin is an instrument inseparable from time, having taken thousands of years of search and refinement to evolve from the applied principle of setting a tightened and taut string vibrating against a hollow background. In fact, both the violin and the bow are derived from the bow and arrow – from the quiver of the string, just audible as it is released, pizzicato, to send the arrow on its path. The violin bow gradually changed shape to become more malleable and was strung with a hundred prickly horsehairs to rub the strings out of their tense and immobile expectancy – but essentially it remained a flexible length of wood. The body of the violin itself was evolved from a hollowed-out length of wood; resonant, no longer as flexible as the bow, but able to trap, amplify and prolong vibrations. Strung with four strings which initiate these vibrations, it transmits them by means of the bridge to the body of the instrument.

The universality of the violin as an instrument of music is illustrated by the fact that our own violin, perfected in Italy in the seventeenth century, has been altogether successfully adopted into cultures as alien as the Indian, where the player squats on the ground with the violin base pressed against his ribs and the violin head pointing diagonally downwards, resting on a tòe. Again, the violin is equally at home among the nomadic, intuitive gypsy peoples, fulfilling yet another, altogether different expressive requirement – wild, natural and nostalgic.

From the fiddlers of the Hardanger plateau in Norway to the Highlands of Scotland, from the urbanised Jews of European Russia to the quaint fiddlers of the Blue Ridge Mountains of the Carolinas, and now on a vast scale to the people of Japan, the violin has succeeded in suiting every style and fulfilling every need.

Let us now consider the peculiar difficulties and requirements of the violin as an instrument to master.

There is no fixed or immovable point of support for the instrument, nor is there any – except for those parts of the feet touching and balancing on the floor – for the violinist himself. The violin must become one with the fluid movement of the whole person, responding visibly to the undulant flow, to the swing, pendulum or circle, never blocking this flow at any of the joints of the body or at any of the points of contact with the violin and bow, and directing it into the very last muscle and finger joint, which must be trained to move in all directions and to control while in motion, as the violinist himself must respond visibly to that inner surge which is born of the music itself and of his thoughts and feelings about it.

Unlike most other instruments and most other activities in general (and unlike, incidentally, the Indian way of playing the violin) the hands, which must be extremely flexible, strong and resilient, are employed wellnigh continually on or around shoulder level, that is above the heart. As they must be continually supplied with blood, the heart must be in good condition and under no strain (or minimal strain) from any causes of anxiety or tension. The problem of maintaining circulation by the follow-up and alternating of movements, efforts, pressures and relaxation; the problem of training the correct reflexes; the problem of warming up each time one sets out to play – in violin playing these become of crucial importance.

The accuracy and precision, the lightning-like adjustment of pitch, sound and stroke, the switch from the minutest, invisible 'inside' motion to the broad sweep of a golfer's swing, require a degree of mastery allowing of almost no margin whatsoever. In addition to this, an intellectual and 'emotional' grasp of the musical work in hand is necessary; and finally, with the quality of grace or inspiration, you have a good performance.

Have I made it all sound unreasonably difficult, the controlling of an instrument so intractable and so infinitely subtle as to be a kind of Untamable Shrew? I hope not, for although the violinist's is a very challenging profession, good violin playing is by no means impossible, and can in fact be a long and deep satisfaction to teach, to learn and to conquer.

To prepare oneself properly for this task, I think it is necessary not only to concentrate on the playing of the violin, but to cultivate an attitude of mind and heart, as well as certain habits of hygiene and general physical condition, so as to burden the playing itself as little as humanly possible with impediments of any kind.

I would like to say a few words about the moral attitude. I look on this as a kind of bridge between the past and the future and between oneself and the outside world. In working, one is investing effort and consolidating memory for the reward of future performance; the better and more precise, the more complete and dedicated the effort, the greater will be the reward. With the equation between oneself and the world at large, we receive as much inspiration from both the music we play and the audience we play to, as we give of ourselves. This conception of a personal budget is valuable for living in general, and underlines the importance of conscience, of example and of integrity and honesty; when we are working on the violin we are alone, and yet what happens during these hours of isolation is crucial to what will happen on the stage before an audience.

Even that cold and clammy word hygiene has its place in the approach to the violin, for health is a very necessary concomitant, and cleanliness, stimulation of the circulation by contrasting temperatures such as hot and cold water, rubbing the skin with a rough glove, as well as certain exertion in sport and other activities alternating with rest, all add to the general toning of muscle and circulation. These are good maxims to bear in mind. Even though violin playing demands infinite subtlety, it also demands great resistance and strength. It is useful to swim, to play tennis even, provided one can relax completely and recapture the subtlest sensations of violin-playing; provided – and this is so personal and individual a reaction that it cannot be made an arbitrary law – it in no way alienates one from the centre of one's being as a violinist, either mentally or physically.

Again, diet is obviously a very important element and one which must be left to the individual in his infinite variety of metabolism and body chemistry; but I would recommend a balanced diet, with plenty of raw fruit and vegetables, and a minimum of fried foods. It is well to avoid foods made with refined flour and refined sugar, especially sweets of the artificial kind, those insidious energisers which together with cigarettes and alcohol give with one hand and take away plus an additional discount with the other. (For the medical support of this principle, see *Nutrition and Physical Degeneration* by Walter D. Price. Also, for additional reading I recommend *The Saccharine Diseases* by T. Cleave.) It is also important never to eat too much food at any time, especially prior to playing.

Ideally violin-playing should begin at the age of three or four as in Russia and more recently in Japan. Two lessons a week – the instruments remaining with the teacher – are sufficient. At that stage the child learns, as all fledglings do, by example and challenge. In my experience, however, by the time a child is eight or nine he or she can grasp the mechanical analyses and explanations quite clearly.

The following texts, which complement the six films (see Publisher's Note), are intended as much for the teacher's use in guiding pupils, as for the older student. The films will help the teacher to encourage even the very youngest, as well as to illustrate to all my basic approach. The words and diagrams printed here aim to provide the firm underpinnings of theory, method and application; my further aim is to furnish additional exercises and means of checking in detail, which it was not possible to include in the restricted time of the films. Several refinements and crystallizations have also taken place since the films were completed, which I did not wish to exclude.

Though this book is organized in six lessons, I do not recommend that the student or the teacher should work through them steadily page by page. The exercises in Lesson I should daily precede all the others. Those in Lessons II and III should be practised concurrently a little every day until the basic elements have been mastered. The more advanced exercises in Lessons IV and V should also be practised concurrently, with a frequent return to Lessons II and III to refresh the basic approach. Lesson VI can be done alone incorporating, as it should, all the others. Finally Appendix I offers some hints on practising, and a series of daily exercises for the advanced violinist.

Sometimes the analysis and the exercises may appear didactic and too specific in their deliberate application to those minute movements, those inner feelings of parts of the fingers, which become, as it were, antennae. My purpose is to develop the utmost sensitivity to the subtlest movements, and to guide the teacher in awakening the pupil to these sensations.

In violin playing it would be wrong to stop at that point, however; for the technique is but the means without which you are helpless, unable to convey your musical conception, however clear it may be, in all its colour and spontaneity. Those movements which I have so carefully classified will ultimately merge into each other and overlap in a manner that not only defies analysis (which at that stage is anyway useless) but will also inevitably contradict one or other of our carefully enunciated dicta. This process, resembling that of digestion, depends largely on the physical characteristics of each individual violinist; therefore the teacher like the gifted doctor must know how to temper and adjust these exercises according to the physical, psychological and emotional attributes of the pupil in front of him.

A violinist's work is never done; but having worked for some fifty years on the instrument, I feel that the time is ripe, for better or worse, to put into words the approach I have evolved. I have tried in these pages to cover what I believe to be the material means essential to violin-playing. I hope that this book will be useful, that it will encourage the study of the violin, and that it will help others to experience the inner joys and satisfactions that the violin has brought to me.

LESSON I

General Preparatory Exercises

I have evolved a technical approach to violin playing, based on a wave or pulse action, which reconciles conflicting impulses and directions in any one continuous activity. Movements are described in terms of ellipses, circles and arcs, all of which partake in this basic action. The conservation of energy as momentum is also essential to my approach. In its conception the method is really quite simple. I hope that this simplicity will never be forgotten, even during detailed work on some of the more intricate movements.

My approach is in several stages. First, an analysis and training of the stresses of the fingers and limbs in each direction; each has its own particular requirements. Thus, in the vertical direction we have to counteract gravity; in the horizontal we have to maintain flow and continuity; and in the lateral we have to maintain swing or the pendulum action – either as in the metronome where the pivot is at the bottom of the bar, or as in a clock, where the pivot is at the top of the bar.

After developing the sensations associated with these movements on the three planes described, we then reconcile the three together so they interpenetrate each other, as it were. There can never be any one movement in violin playing in which there is not some small part of the others involved, if only as a passive readiness to move in one of the other directions.

The wave action not only reconciles opposing forces by its ebb and flow, but also holds within itself the alternation of the active impulse and the passive momentum, the alternation of tension and relaxation. Within each cycle of movement there is a moment of minimum effort and a point of perfect balance – I would call it the zero point.

In developing technique, whether in the left hand or the right hand, there are three stages. The first stage is a complete softness of the joints, as in a baby, each checked separately. The second stage is the co-ordination of soft movements and the development of elasticity and resilience, both in stretching and compressing actions. The third and final stage is the development of strength and firmness, and freedom. These stages cannot occur in any other order. If, for instance, firmness precedes elasticity, there are dire results in terms of stiffness. Again, if elasticity precedes the feeling of complete softness and passivity, there is bound to be a residue of tension. A violinist must always be prepared to take the three stages in their correct sequence whenever he picks up his instrument.

The advantage of the resistance exercises which I have evolved lies in their cumulative effect. Each side opposing the other is strengthened by this very opposition. Without any visible movement great strength can be developed. The

16

measure of your sense of well-being can be gauged by the energy of the two opposing forces which check and balance each other within you.

In the very first standing pose you can exercise nearly every muscle in your body, remaining all the while quite still. This form of exercise is one of the secrets of resilience and strength.

One essential foundation of violin playing is a good posture, and you must first of all discover the most natural stance which will easily absorb and accommodate the various movements of the body associated with playing the violin.

Posture thought of in itself seems a static situation. This is by no means the case. Not only is it the result of a continuous balance of opposing forces, but at the same time it is imbued with pulse and rhythm, the pulse of our heart and the rhythm of our breathing. I would like to begin this exposition on violin technique with a word on breathing.

Breathing

Life begins with breathing, and it is something so basic to all activity and to all musical art that it is essential to be aware of it while practising. Breathing should be smooth and unforced, and even during the most intricate movements involved in playing the violin it should continue quietly. A certain amount of training and a high degree of co-ordination are necessary to achieve this. We will learn about co-ordination in the following lessons. At this point I would like to define good breathing and to give you a few basic exercises.

Good breathing requires the ability to inhale and exhale evenly, i.e. the same time should be taken in both inhalation and exhalation. The period for each inhalation and exhalation should be as long as possible. Some Indians have developed this to such an extent that they can take four minutes on an inhalation and four minutes on an exhalation. I believe some pearl divers have managed to hold their breaths at least that long, but this is not what we are after. In violin playing we need continuous breathing, and we must never hold our breath (although as an exercise careful unforced breath retention is of benefit).

Perhaps the best initial exercise is to sit on the ground with legs folded upon each other, hands (palms upwards) resting on the knees, spine straight, neck and shoulders relaxed, chest free and held high, and to begin breathing quietly. A watch is useful to count the seconds of each inhalation and exhalation. Try to prolong the length of each without getting out of breath.

A further exercise which greatly increases the control of the lung capacity is to place the right hand over the nose, blocking the right nostril with the tip of the thumb, and the left nostril with the tip or nail of the third finger (see Diagram 1). Release the left nostril just

Diagram 1

17

enough to allow a very thin column of air to enter. (a) Inhale through the left nostril; (b) exhale through the right nostril by releasing the thumb ever so slightly, while closing the left nostril with the second finger – exhale completely; (c) inhale through the right nostril; (d) exhale through the left.

The skill of this exercise is measured by the length of each inhalation and exhalation, by the narrowness of the aperture through which the air passes in the nostril, and by the silence of this air passage. If you can inhale for 45 seconds and exhale for another 45 seconds, and do the complete cycle ten times, you will have good control over your breathing.

Posture and stretching exercises

One of the most difficult features of the violin is that merely *holding* it in playing position can easily inhibit free movement and encourage an unnatural posture. All too often the player then forces a way through these difficulties by sheer determination to an apparent, not a real freedom. The violin is not meant merely to be held, but to be played upon and played with. The ability to adjust movements continuously is the secret of violin playing.

The preparatory exercises in this lesson are done without the instrument, so that when you first pick up the violin or bow, you will have already experienced to some extent the freedom of movement which it will be your goal to achieve in playing. These exercises should be done barefoot and in shorts.

The basis of a good posture is an upward stretching from the toes through the spine to the crown of the head, in which our muscles counteract the natural collapsing tendency of the joints as they surrender to the force of gravity. This erect position is as much a sign of good health in violin playing, as it is of vitality and good health in life.

To describe the maximum vertical stretch, let us begin with the feet (see Diagram 2).

The violinist's weight should fall slightly more on the balls of the feet than on the heels. This forward balance allows for greater mobility and lightness, and enhances the playing position. The arches of the feet should be raised by rolling slightly on to the outside edge of the feet, keeping the toes relaxed (1). This raised position of the arches should be retained when the feet are returned to their normal position by an inward pressure from the ankles (2). The knees are pushed back (3), maintaining the separation of the thighs, while the buttocks are tensed and thrust forward (4). The stomach is

Diagram 2

pulled in and the small of the back held back (5). The chest is pushed forward and upwards diagonally (6) and the head pulled up and back, lengthening the neck (7). Only the shoulders maintained at their horizontal width are completely relaxed and falling, arms, hands and fingers dangling loosely almost parallel to the spine, the rest of the body stretching as if the head were trying to touch the ceiling, and the toes, ball of foot and heels to push the ground away (8). These adjustments, in defiance of gravity, should be done on an inhalation, or, if the breathing is untrained and the adjustments take too long in the beginning, on several inhalations.

On this inhalation the chest reaches its furthest expansion. But you should not let the level of the chest drop on exhaling, for it is against this ballooning fullness that we let the back relax and the shoulders relax, allowing them to move easily forward (as with the right shoulder in certain down-bows) and back (as in certain up-bows).

Having held this taut position for a few moments, go to the other extreme, allowing the body to sag and slump. Alternate several times between the upright and the relaxed posture. This will help you capture the feeling of the various opposing directions of muscular activity as shown in Diagram 2. When you finally retain the erect posture, you can relax the muscles to a certain extent without losing the correct stance. The correct muscle-tone will allow you to retain this stance without strain.

Diagram 3

Basic positions preparatory to action

The first position is what might be called the Muslim prayer position. The legs are folded under the trunk, with the buttocks resting on the heels; the forearms, elbows touching the knees, and the forehead rest on the floor (see Diagram 3). In this position, the body is prepared for action like a spring – the opposite of the 'dead' pose, lying on the back, stretched out and unwound after action. Stretch the shoulders down and forwards, arch the back and then, without raising shins or forearms from the floor roll forward on the head, stretching the back of the neck.

Rise to an upright kneeling position with the back straight, arms hanging down by your sides. Stretch the head and shoulders backwards, hollowing the back and bringing the chest forward while holding the heels with the hands.

19

After these two basic and complementary exercises, we are now ready to take up the next positions, supported by our feet.

Continuous series of stretching exercises

Begin in a crouched position with the body relaxed, the head hanging forwards and the backs of the hands resting on the floor. Take time to feel all your body, by stretching from within the particular muscular part concerned: stretch the shoulder-blades apart; stretch the spine; feel the inner arching of your feet; feel your thumbs and fingers. Try inverting the hands so that the stretched palms and fingers lie flat on the floor. From time to time hold the soles of your feet with your hands and pull, stretching the back more. Take a few deep breaths and, on an exhalation, straighten the legs to a taut stiffness, but keep the head hanging and the hands still touching the floor. Interlock

Diagram 4

your fingers, and put the joined hands behind the head where the neck and head join. Pull the head down. Drop the hands, take a few more breaths, and then, on an inhalation, reach a standing position.

Diagram 5

Exhale and check your posture (refer to Diagram 1). The feet should be parallel, their arches actively felt, the knees straight, the stomach pulled in, the back straight (it is a common fault in violinists to allow the small of the back to become hollow) and the head high. It is important that the shoulders are neither forced back nor down, but are allowed to hang loosely.

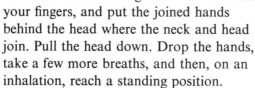

While inhaling again, bring the arms up from your sides to a horizontal position in front of you. Exhale, and stretch the arms forward and out from the shoulders and shoulder-blades. During the next inhalation, bring the arms to an outstretched position above your head while stretching up on your toes. Exhale and bring the palms together (Diagram 6). Press the palms hard together, then move the head back and try to bring the inner sides of the elbows together. Inhale and stretch the arms out sideways at a 45° angle. Exhale and let the arms fall back into the shoulder-blades. Repeat this movement of stretching out from, and falling back into the shoulder-blades several times, at this 45° angle.

Diagram 6   Next, with the arms outstretched horizontally to each side, twist the

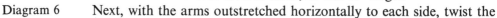

20

elbows. In this movement the hands are kept still with the palms facing the ground, while the arms are rotated in the shoulder sockets; stretch the palms and fingers (Diagram 7a and b). This movement is then combined with stretching and rolling the shoulders forward with each arm alternately, turning the head in the direction of the stretched arm (while the other arm held horizontally relaxes); then do a complementary movement of turning the head away from whichever arm is stretched and rotating (Diagram 8a and b). Next, roll both arms and shoulders forward at the same time, making circles. Pull the head back as the shoulders go forward, and push it forward as the shoulders go back.

In all the preceding exercises do not allow the hands to rotate with the arms; the palms should remain facing downwards, fingers widest and most stretched at the moment of maximum arm rotation.

Diagram 7

(a)　　　(b)

Diagram 8

(a)　　　(b)

Further head exercises

1. Turn the head from side to side and stretch the neck. You may help by pulling the back of the head diagonally with the right hand when the head is turned right, and vice versa.
2. Tilt the head backwards and forwards.
3. Keep the head and chin at the same level and push the head backwards and forwards from the neck (like a chicken).
4. Roll the head in full circles clockwise and anti-clockwise.

Balancing (stork) exercises

Standing on the left foot, hold the right ankle with the right hand, pulling the leg into a bent position as in Diagram 9. Stretch the arm by pulling the ankle and extend the left arm horizontally. Check your posture, rise on the left toes, and hold this position while breathing two or three cycles in and out. You will notice that to maintain balance, the body inclines to the left. Do the same exercise standing on the right foot.

Standing on the right foot, hold the instep of the left foot with the left hand (Diagram 10). Extend the right arm horizontally, and push out and back with the left leg. This pulls the shoulder backwards instead of only down. Do the same exercise standing on the left foot.

Standing on the right foot, hold the left-foot toes with the left-hand fingers, and stretch the leg forward horizontally, as in Diagram 11. This pulls the shoulder forward. Do the same exercise standing on the left foot.

Standing on the left foot, hold the right toes with the right-hand fingers; pull and bend the right leg upwards, knee against stomach, and stretch the right arm alternately on either side of the bent leg. Do the same standing on the right foot.

Try the same exercise standing on the left foot, but holding the right toes with the left hand, so that the right foot is brought across the front of the left leg. Do the same exercise again standing on the right foot; and then try the earlier exercises in the same way, right foot held by left hand, and vice versa. With practice you will be able to do these exercises in one continuous movement, changing smoothly from one to another.

Swinging exercises basic to violin playing

From the very beginning you should feel that your whole body is prepared to participate in the act of playing, either initiating movement or sympathetically responding to it, even to the subtlest invisible movements which echo to the violin's and the bow's own vibrations. The next series of exercises will enable you to come closer to the sensations of playing, although their full application to the violin will only come at a later stage in Lessons IV, V and VI.

The habit of readiness in the whole body should be cultivated; obviously when you play you will not make such an extreme movement as in these exercises, although there are certain strokes at times that demand quite a wide swing of the body.

So far, your feet have been kept together, but in playing the violin they should be far enough apart to form a solid yet flexible base for balance, though near enough together to allow you to transfer your weight easily from one leg to the other. They should therefore be approximately 12 in. apart, and turned very slightly outwards – the exact distance will depend on the body-build and the length of the legs of the individual concerned.

On this wider base, while maintaining even weight on both legs, practise shifting this weight from one leg to the other. Then rotate the body first to one side and then the other on a horizontal plane – arms dangling and then flying out during each

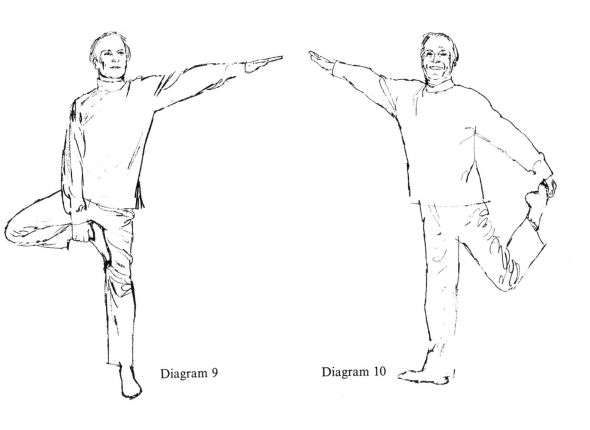

Diagram 9

Diagram 10

Diagram 11

Lesson I

rotation – moving each time when in the extreme position on to the opposite foot. The momentum thus caught pushes you into the reverse direction.

Now we come to the co-ordinated circles of the arms which I hope will lead to good violin playing. We will begin them in their easiest and most natural position, i.e. hanging loosely.

Let the upper part of the body hang down from the waist, so that the finger-tips touch the floor, the legs being kept straight, the head hanging down. By pushing your weight slightly from one foot to the other, begin a gentle sway of the body setting the arms in motion, so that the finger-tips describe circles on the floor. (Notice that the circles are in opposite directions and alternate.) Keep the swinging motion going in the whole body and rise gradually to a standing position, the arms being carried to a violin playing position. The wrists and fingers should remain soft enough to participate in the wave motion of the upper limbs. The neck should also be relaxed, allowing the head to roll with the body-swing.

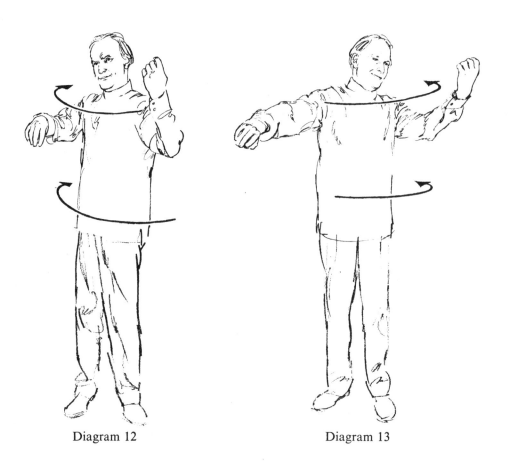

Diagram 12   Diagram 13

24

The next exercise is for the shoulders and the muscles of the back and is not connected with the previous one. Stretch the arms out sideways, parallel to the floor, keeping the shoulders down. Let the forearms drop from the elbows. In order for the forearms to hang really vertically, the shoulders must roll forward. Keep this right angle between the forearm and upper arm and swing the forearms up from their vertical hanging position to a vertical upright position. Repeat this movement several times.

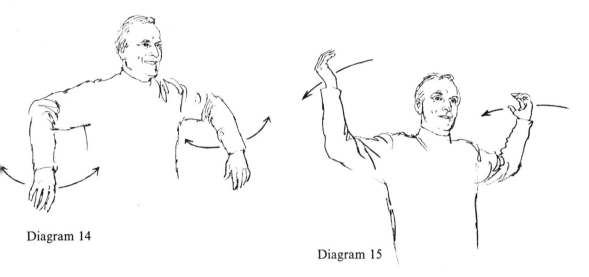

Diagram 14

Diagram 15

Place the left arm in violin playing position, the forearm at approximately a 45° angle to the body, the wrist loose. By allowing the elbow to swing from side to side and the forearm to move backwards and forwards, make a circular movement with the left hand on a horizontal plane. Place the right arm in the same position, and describe circles with both hands simultaneously, first clockwise, then anti-clockwise. Move the right arm into its own playing position, palm of the hand downwards, and make circular movements with each hand in opposite directions. In this position the right hand will describe anti-clockwise ellipses on a nearly horizontal plane, and the left hand will describe clockwise circles, the forearm pivoting and swinging upon the elbow.

Stand on your toes, stretch the arms high above the head, palms facing outwards, and swing both arms backwards and forwards. On each hand-swing backwards straighten the knees and cave in the back simultaneously, with shoulder-blades back and the head back.

Try to feel the different speeds of these unforced natural swings of the arms according to the longer or shorter distance from the hand to the shoulder. You will notice that if each of the swings described is completely relaxed, it has its own natural speed. Until you become aware of this, there will be some residual tension in the arm and shoulder, or you will be deliberately moving them.

25

Lesson I

I would now like to explain the principles of *thrust* and *momentum*.

In ellipses of every description and circular swings having a vertical component, there is always one point of maximum speed – the moment of greatest thrust. This occurs naturally at the approach to the lowest point, but can be artificially applied at any point along the path.

In playing the violin we must become aware of that instant of maximum thrust in each repeated movement – it may precede the moment of maximum speed if deliberately applied. After that moment the remainder of the movement continues in passive relaxation, using the momentum gathered.

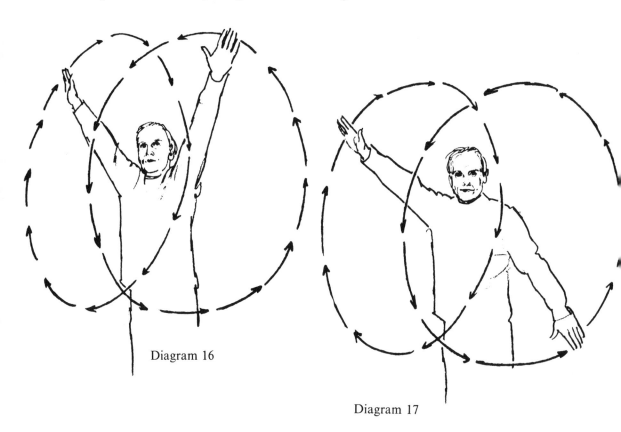

Diagram 16

Diagram 17

In the next exercise the arms are straightened. With a full arm rotation, make circles right from the shoulder, letting the arms cross in front of you, each in turn above the other. This should be done several times, first with an outward impulse of the arms, then with an inward impulse, taking care to develop an awareness of the thrust and momentum principles. Try the exercise in two pairs of directions.

The above movements should be done again, but this time with the impulses occurring one after the other, not simultaneously. Do not neglect the rhythmic pulse in the elbow joints, wrists and fingers, the latter reaching their maximum spread and stretched position at the moment when the arm is at its longest.

Swing both arms simultaneously in the same circular direction, first clockwise then anti-clockwise (Diagram 18).

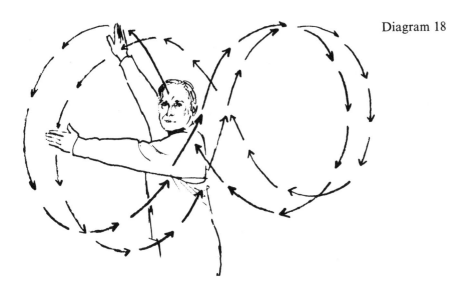

Diagram 18

You have seen how this movement can be co-ordinated in two parallel and two opposite directions, thus giving four choices in all.

Finally, swing the arms in front of you, each in the shape of a figure 8 lying on its side (∞), allowing them to bend, the joints moving more freely. This combines a down-bow and an up-bow in each figure 8. In the down-bow, the fingers and thumbs should be open and spread. At the extreme point of the down-bow and of the up-bow you should feel the movement in the shoulder-blades.

Diagram 19

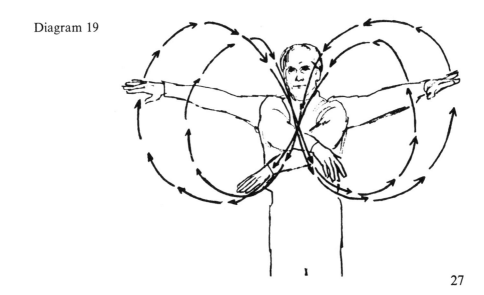

Lesson I

Not to forget the legs, stand on one leg, arms held out horizontally, and swing the other like a pendulum as vigorously and in as wide an arc as possible, accommodating this movement with a swinging of the body and the arms. The body and the arms should swing clockwise as the right leg is thrown forward, and in the opposite direction as the left leg is thrown forward.

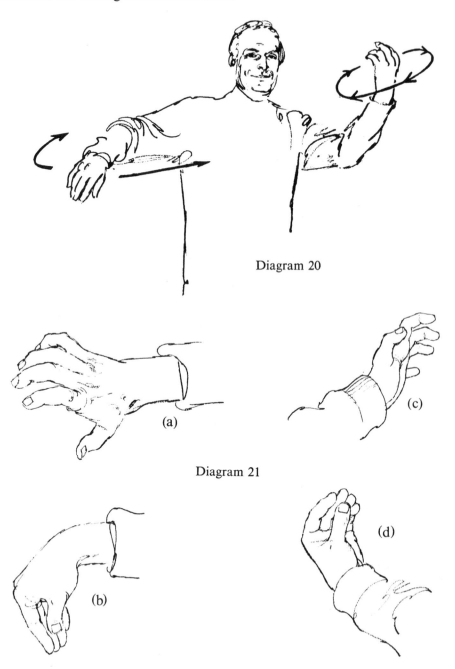

Diagram 20

(a)

(c)

Diagram 21

(b)

(d)

For our last swinging exercise we will do the one that comes nearest to actual violin playing. Lift the left forearm to the raised position, which is illustrated in Diagram 20; fingers and wrist should be free and elbow able to swing. The right palm should face downwards as when bowing, and again with fingers and wrist completely soft and free. With the right arm slightly bent, begin your swing action which will set both arms, including wrists and fingers, in motion. To simulate violin playing more accurately and come nearer to the actual sensation, be guided by the following indications, illustrated in Diagram 21:

(a) When right arm is outstretched, fingers spread.
(b) When right arm bends, fingers draw together and fold up as the movement continues.
(c) When left hand is thrown away from body (in violin playing position), fingers gather together.
(d) When left hand is thrown towards body, fingers spread.

(a) and (c) can happen simultaneously in concurrent swings of both arms. Therefore naturally (b) and (d) also happen together. Further, (a) and (d) can happen simultaneously, and, by the same token, also (b) and (c).

Five yoga exercises

To end this lesson here are some yoga exercises, the first four of which should be held for at least three breathing cycles.

1. Press the palms together against the spine, first as in Diagram 22 and then as in Diagram 23. The shoulder-blades are pulled back, and the arms and the hands are pushed together and upwards.

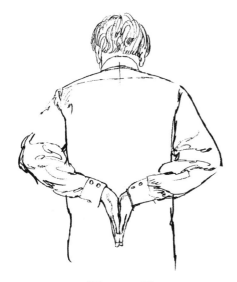

Diagram 22   Diagram 23

Diagram 25

Diagram 24   Diagram 26

2. *The shoulder stand* or *neck balance*. The body is vertical, the hands pressed firmly against the back (see Diagram 24). The chest should be pushed out, the chin' pressing against it. This position can be tried first against a wall.

3. *Plough Pose*. If you wish to hold the position for a long time (which is extremely beneficial), it may be easier to rest the feet on a chair. The 'plough pose' (see Diagram 25) lends itself to a number of variations whereby the hands can resist the feet in different ways. The palms can touch and try to push the feet apart. They can also push the feet together from the outside. They can try to push the legs up and to pull the legs down. These are all useful variations.

4. Having done the 'plough' exercises which bend the back in a convex shape, it is a good idea to bend the back in the opposite way – in the concave. This can be done on the floor, lying on one's back, bending the legs and holding the ankles with the hands while you raise the back off the floor into an arched shape (see Diagram 26). The maximum back-bend is achieved by placing the hands, palms on floor, behind the head, fingers pointing towards feet, and lifting the head and body completely off the floor, except for the feet and hands.

30

5. Finally, the delicious pay-off; after these variations of stretching and resistance, etc., lie on the floor completely outstretched in utter relaxation. The greater the effort which precedes, the more enjoyable this phase will be. It is in fact called the 'dead pose'. When this pose is completely relaxed, you can feel the pulse of the circulation of the blood in the arms (the forearms particularly), and sometimes if you are completely relaxed, even in the legs.

Breathing quietly, concentrate on releasing all tension limb by limb and joint by joint, feeling the heaviness of each as if sinking into the floor. You can remain like this for twenty minutes or more if you have the time.

Diagram 27

LESSON II

Preparatory Exercises – Right Hand

I think it is easier at first to use a round wooden stick (light and unvarnished, about 1½–2 ft. in length and roughly the diameter of the bow) in these exercises. When the sensations have become more familiar and you have tried the Preliminary Exercises with the Bow (p. 40), you should then repeat the earlier exercises substituting the bow itself for the stick.

Balance of the stick at its middle point and position of fingers

Support the end of the stick with the left hand. With right arm bent at elbow and with the forearm approximately parallel to the floor, hold the stick at its middle balancing point, using the thumb and second finger only. They should both be soft and rounded so that the right-hand top corner of the thumb and thumb-nail touch the stick, and a circle is completed by the second finger touching the stick diagonally across its first joint. Add the other fingers lightly – first the fourth finger, its tip resting not quite on the top of the stick but just on the inside, then the first finger resting somewhat on its side just between its first and second joint, and finally the third finger touching between its pad and its first joint.

The fingers should be rounded and evenly spaced (not touching each other). The hand should hang slightly from the wrist and should be soft.

You will notice that the distance between the point where the fingers touch the stick and where they join the hand is greater in the fourth finger than in the first.

Diagram 2

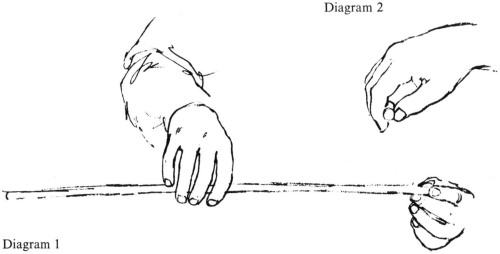

Diagram 1

This means that the knuckles are at a slight angle to the stick and not exactly parallel to it. This angle is exploited and continually adjusted through the rotation and slight raising of the right arm.

Balance of the stick in playing position

With the left hand gradually pull the stick little by little leftwards through your fingers, letting go with the left hand often enough so that your fourth finger becomes sensitive to its increasing responsibility for the extra support needed to balance the stick. The pulling of the stick with the left hand is a substitute for the resistance of the violin strings, and the letting go brings about a state which in actual playing corresponds to the carrying of the bow in the air, off the string, or to the balancing of the bow when playing in its lower half. Keep the other fingers soft throughout, and be aware that no trace of a 'grip' is used to carry the weight of the stick, even when it is supported by the left hand.

Co-ordinated movements of thumb, fingers and knuckles

These will be easier to learn if you keep in mind the idea that the hold of the bow is made up of two main 'shapes' – a ring or *circle* and an arch or *bridge* (referred to in the film as two arcs). The first is the circle formed by the thumb and second finger when you first balanced and held the stick at its middle point (Diagram 3). The second shape is the bridge which consists of the knuckles supported by two *piers*: one being the first finger which is able to apply weight from either side of the stick; the other, a two-legged one, comprising the third and fourth fingers which exert pressure on either side of the stick (Diagram 4). (The specific application of this will be dealt with later.)

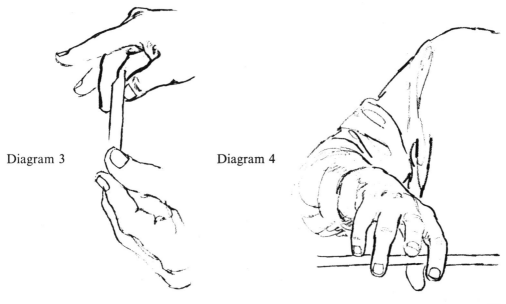

Diagram 3   Diagram 4

Lesson II

Although the weight of the arm is directed mainly to the first finger, the particular importance of this bridge lies in a spreading movement which distributes some of the weight back to the third and fourth fingers and involves them in active participation in the stroke.

THE CIRCLE

Still holding the stick with the left hand, slide the right thumb forwards and backwards along it, without moving the rest of the hand and making sure that the top right-hand corner of the thumb remains in contact with the stick. Thus the thumb should bend when sliding along the stick to the left (towards the tip) and straighten somewhat when sliding to the right (towards the nut), though never enough to lose a slight outward curve. (The bending of the thumb as it slides towards the tip of the bow coincides with a clockwise rolling of the bow, and as it slides towards the nut with an anti-clockwise bow roll. Thus every movement is to a certain extent affected, and sometimes even contradicted, by associated movements.) The other fingers should also keep their point of contact with the stick and the hand should be hanging slightly from the wrist.

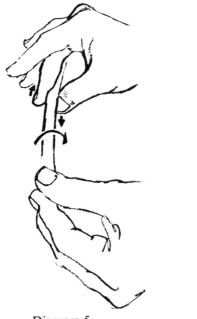

Diagram 5

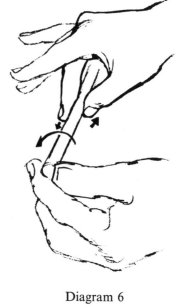

Diagram 6

Now take the first, third and fourth fingers off the stick and once again slide the thumb. This time, make the second finger slide in a contrary direction to the thumb – to the nut when the thumb slides to the tip and vice versa. You will notice the stick inclining alternately to the left and right (see Diagrams 5 and 6). Once again, and indeed in all the exercises on the bow, make sure that none of the points of contact change.

34

When the combination of the two movements begins to feel natural, stop the thumb and second finger actually sliding along the stick, but retain their opposing pressures, which results in a slight waving of the stick, light as it is, while the bending and straightening of the thumb is still clearly visible.

In its basic position the thumb is well bent in a horizontal direction and the muscle at its base remains soft. This position is associated with the following:

(a) The initial part of the down-bow stroke;

(b) String-crossing to an upper string; for example

(c) The immediate anticipation of a down-bow stroke at the end of an up-bow;

(d) Very short up-bow strokes such as re-takes, flying staccato or spiccato (in which the anticipation of the following stroke is about as long as the stroke itself).

In its second position the thumb is slightly less bent and the muscle at its base becomes active. This position is associated with the following:

(a) General up-bow direction;

(b) String-crossing to a lower string;

(c) The immediate anticipation of an up-bow stroke at the end of a down-bow;

(d) Very short down-bow strokes (in which the following up-bow stroke is anticipated).

By modifying the bending and straightening of the thumb in the vertical direction, you can also *roll* the stick (see Diagrams 5 and 6 opposite). This movement, used in combination with up- and down-bow strokes, alters the angle of the bow-hair to the string, anti-clockwise on the approach to the nut in up-bows (wrist rises), and clockwise on the approach to the tip in down-bows (wrist falls). It is also associated with varying the distance of the bow from the bridge to effect changes of tone, colour and dynamics.

(In describing clockwise and anti-clockwise rolls of the bow, it is assumed that the observer is viewing the bow from the nut end, looking squarely from behind the nut down the whole length of the stick to the point.)

THE BRIDGE

Holding the end of the stick with the left hand, place the first, third and fourth fingers on the stick and now remove the thumb and second finger. In both the down-bow and the up-bow the piers tend to push away from each other. This feeling can best be developed if at first you allow the piers actually to slide on the stick, though eventually they will remain anchored to the bow. In the down-bow when the piers separate, the knuckles and wrist are lowered and the elbow rises slightly. In the up-bow when the piers separate, the knuckles and wrist are raised and the elbow drops very slightly. (See Diagrams 7 and 8 respectively.)

In both cases it is most important to feel the spreading apart of the fingers and knuckles, even while the fingers slightly 'gather' in the up-bow. It is essential that there be an instant of complete relaxation between these two successive 'firmish' sensations.

Now alternate between down- and up-bow sensations, passing each time through a

Diagram 7

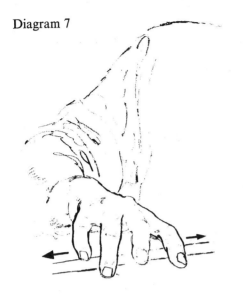

Diagram 8

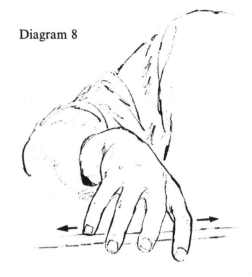

Diagram 9

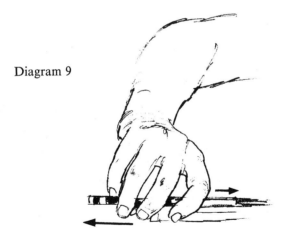

Diagram 10

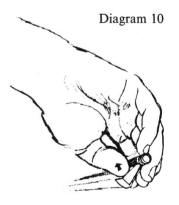

'zero' stage in which the spreading effort of the hand is released. It is important that an equal effort be made by both piers. Whenever one is allowed to be lazier or more energetic we are in danger of establishing a bad habit.

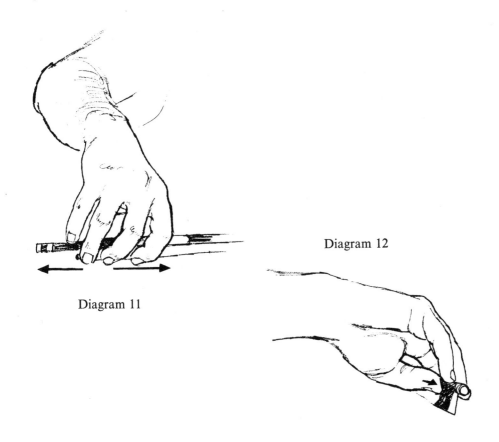

Diagram 12

Diagram 11

COMBINATION OF CIRCLE AND BRIDGE

Continuing the above alternating spreading movements, you will now add the movements of the thumb and second finger. At first these movements should be practised on the stick, and later on the bow, as illustrated in Diagrams 9 and 10. In the down-bow when the knuckles are lowered, the thumb bends, pressing towards the tip of the bow like the first finger, while the second finger joins the third and fourth fingers pressing towards the nut. In the up-bow when the knuckles are raised, the thumb this time joins the third and fourth fingers in pressing towards the nut, while the second finger is now allied to the first, pressing towards the tip (Diagrams 11 and 12). Take care that none of the movements preceding or to come disturb the point of contact between the stick and each finger or the thumb.

The combination of the movements can also be practised without the stick. Be careful that your attention is not so exclusively focused on your hands that you fail to notice possible unwanted tensions in the upper arm and shoulder.

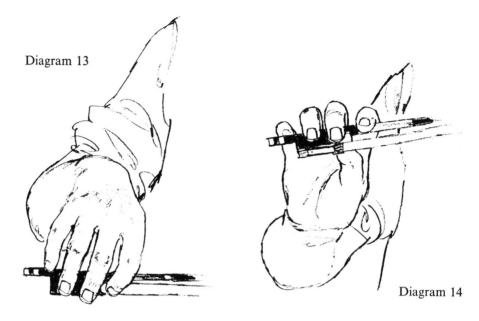

Diagram 13

Diagram 14

Flexibility and softness of the fingers and thumb when carrying the stick unsupported by the left hand

FINGERS MOVING VERTICALLY

Let us now return to our very first hold of the stick at its middle point, where it is automatically balanced in the right hand alone. Keeping the hand and arm still, raise the stick as far as possible by bending the fingers and thumb; then, straightening the fingers and thumb, lower the stick. When the stick is raised, it rolls in a clockwise direction; when lowered, it rolls in an anti-clockwise direction. As usual, take care that the points of contact do not change. As soon as you have achieved the maximum movement of the fingers (and thus of the stick) you may add the movement of the hand to that of the fingers, moving it up and down from the wrist to increase the distance the stick travels.

Repeat these movements, gradually moving the hand up the stick towards the nut, so that you become aware of the role of the fourth finger in balancing the stick without losing its flexibility (Diagrams 13 and 14).

To increase your flexibility and adaptability, try – as a matter of curiosity – waving the stick with your hand and releasing the third and fourth fingers on each upward swing of the hand, allowing the fingers to touch the stick as it nears its lowest point.

FINGERS MOVING HORIZONTALLY

As we are largely concerned with continuous horizontal movement in violin playing, our fingers must learn to be flexible in this direction.

Hold the stick at the nut in the neutral position, supported by the softest possible hold of the fingers and thumb. Now push and pull the bow with the left hand, increasing the pressure of the hold just enough to ensure that the stick does not slip through fingers and thumb. These, however, should all remain flexible enough to respond passively to the push and pull, simulating the up-bow and down-bow, straightening in the former, bending in the latter (Diagrams 15 and 16).

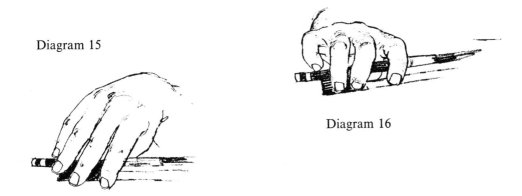

Diagram 15

Diagram 16

Now hold the stick vertically with the right hand alone, and push it up by simultaneously bending the fingers and raising the hand from the wrist. Then let the hand and fingers be sensitive enough to gravity to allow the stick to fall, its weight pulling the hand down and straightening the fingers. Here, the fourth finger gradually comes off the stick and the third hardly touches it (Diagrams 17 and 18).

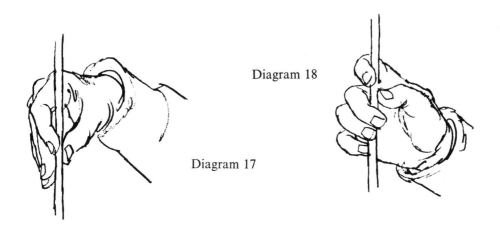

Diagram 18

Diagram 17

To feel the same sensation in the opposite direction, invert the stick and repeat the above exercise, only this time the active lift will come from straightening the fingers upwards and the passive fall will bend them.

The preceding exercises are a preparation for achieving the same flexibility when the bow is horizontal and the fingers actively bend to the left and straighten to the right – which movements you should now try.

CIRCLES (Combination of the vertical and horizontal finger movements)
When you have mastered both the vertical and horizontal finger movements (with the stick horizontal), you should be ready to combine them in a circle in either direction. This circular movement should be practised with the stick held at various angles between the vertical and the horizontal. All the fingers should work equally so that both ends of the stick describe the same-sized circle. The impulse for this movement should come from the arm.

Even at this early stage, experiment in doing the previous exercises while holding the stick balanced with only the first and second fingers against the thumb. You will find that the second finger takes on some of the duties of the third and fourth, but keep it as close to the thumb as possible. It may possibly have to roll up and down the stick a little. To keep first and second fingers really loose while doing this, the arm needs to be turned well inwards, so that the first finger lies on the stick on the joint between the base and middle phalange.

Preliminary exercises with the bow

We now exchange the stick for the bow itself. The following exercise is helpful in giving an idea of the range of movement required in actual bowing, without the full weight of the bow having to be supported.

The nut of the bow is placed on a music stand, as shown in Diagram 19. The tip is held by the left hand. The right hand is then placed lightly on the bow at the heel. The only element of hold in this placing of the hand is the feeling of contact in the 'circle' between second finger and thumb, which should be formed loosely before placing the hand on the bow. The hand then falls naturally into a comfortable position. This feeling of contact in the 'circle' should be maintained as the hand slides up the stick all the way to the point and back again. The arm should be so light and poised that there is no feeling of pull against this hold. One should remember that the shoulder and shoulder-blade follow the hand and fingers in a down-bow and conversely make room for the hand path in an up-bow. As there is next to no momentum in this soft glide, there will be hardly any visible finger movement beyond the slight difference in inclination between up- and down-bow, a difference which, given a really soft hand, will happen by itself through the action of friction between fingers and bow-stick.

A further re-active movement which should appear in this exercise is the compensatory adjustment of angles between upper arm, forearm, wrist and fingers, which keeps the bow parallel with the bridge. This adjustment, which we shall be considering in more detail later on, begins at the moment the arm starts moving and continues right through the stroke. As shown in Diagrams 20 and 21, the varying planes in which the arm has to move in order to bow on the different strings can be simulated by altering the height at which the heel is supported and by tilting the tip of the bow.

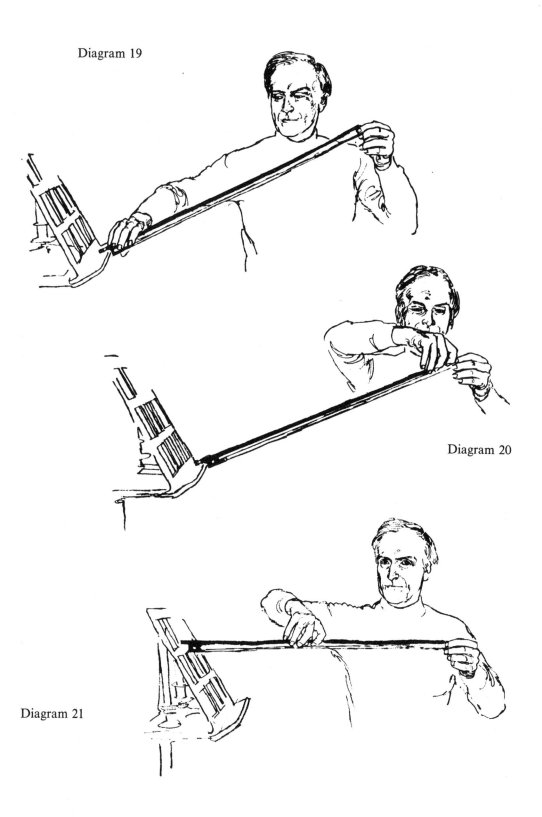

Diagram 19

Diagram 20

Diagram 21

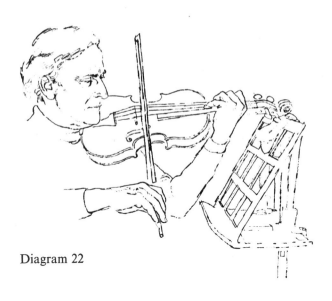

Diagram 22

Diagram 23

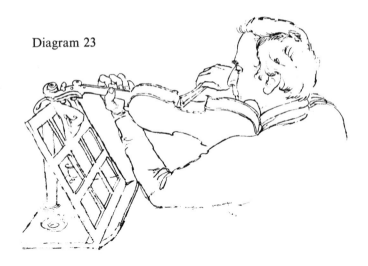

Balancing the bow

When the bow is actually held and carried, these natural adjustments can be blocked by excess tension in wrist, fingers and thumb which transmits itself up the arm to the shoulder, locking the whole limb solid. The exercises which follow are mainly designed to bring about from the very start a basic bow-hold which allows these and all other necessary re-active movements full play. At the same time they accustom the hand, particularly the little finger and thumb, to the widely differing degrees of muscle-tone which are appropriate to the different bowing functions. A further aim of these exercises, which will be continued in more elaborate form in Lesson IV, is the promotion of a feeling for the elasticity of the bow and the effect on this of varying degrees of elasticity in the joints.

For these exercises it is necessary to support the violin in a simulated playing position as shown in Diagrams 22 and 23, which enables the left arm to experience from the start the sensation of freedom that it should always maintain in playing, and the left-hand fingers to develop strength.

We start off with the middle of the bow supported by one of the strings. We take off second and third fingers, holding as lightly as possible with the remaining ones, first finger, fourth finger and thumb. We then press down the fourth finger until the bow leaves the string. (This exercise completely loses its point if the bow is lifted by any other means than this fourth finger pressure.) As well as lifting the bow, this pressure will result in a further rounding of the thumb and a folding upwards of the first finger, which should not however grip on to the stick.

The bow is thus poised above the string for a few moments; then the pressure on the fourth finger is released, the bow falls back on to the string and is allowed to bounce, with the hand absolutely relaxed, until it comes to rest of its own accord. If the hand has really let go, then the bounces will be felt to 'echo' in the hand and up the whole arm.

In the second stage of the exercise, which produces a real ricochet effect, at the moment of release of pressure the bow is drawn quite slowly towards the tip until it reaches a point at which the bounces peter out. (Players with arms of normal length should not go too near the tip because this bow-hold is unsuitable for that part of the bow.) Then, by means of pressure from the little finger, the bow is raised again, carried back to its starting point and dropped once more. As a variant, instead of carrying the bow back to its starting point, one can release the bow from above the point reached after the down-bow, and draw the bow back towards the heel, producing an up-bow ricochet. How far the bounces continue on the up-bow depends on the lightness in arm and shoulder, which is an essential pre-condition of this exercise.

This second stage exercise should then be repeated with all the fingers on the bow. One should feel that, in the carried state, the second and third fingers are actively helping, particularly the second, because the 'circle' is in action again. In the released, bouncing state, however, the second and third fingers should share in feeling the bouncing without in any way impeding it. The ricochet should sound the same whether the middle fingers are on the stick or not.

If after a few days of practising these ricochet exercises it is found that the little finger retains the rather common tendency to 'cave in' under pressure, the following toning-up exercise is often helpful. As in preparation for the ricochet exercise, the bow is raised from the string by fourth finger pressure, but instead of being dropped on to the string by releasing the pressure, it is lowered as gently and *slowly* as possible, coming to rest silently without a quiver.

Lesson II

String-crossing movement

A further exercise to be practised with the violin supported as in Diagrams 22 and 23 involves resting the tip of the bow on the G string for a few moments, and then allowing the whole arm in one piece to drop down so that the tip rests on the E string. The bow is then lightly lifted up to the G string level again. This exercise should be repeated at the middle of the bow and at the heel, where a relatively untrained little finger will become acutely aware of its balancing function. (At this early stage, it should be stressed that the crossing at the heel should be made with the whole arm moving in one piece, without any independent movement of wrist and/or fingers. In Lesson IV, however, we will discuss the advantages of staggering the movements of hand and arm in string-crossing at the heel.)

Whole bows with free-swinging arm

We are now in a position to combine the free-swinging arm, as experienced in the exercises illustrated in Diagrams 18 and 19 in Lesson I (p. 27), with our ability to carry the bow without stiffening.

First, without violin or bow, we modify the curves produced in the exercises in Lesson I, in accordance with our feeling for the planes in which the arm moves in actual bowing. We imagine that we are producing a fairly fast up-bow followed by a slowish return in the air. Starting with right arm fully extended, we swing it vigorously leftwards and upwards as if drawing the bow towards the heel. The movement is however followed through well beyond the imaginary heel, until the right-hand knuckles are about on a level with the left ear. If both wrist and fingers are in a soft state, they will now be folded leftwards and upwards in an extension of the arm movement. We then change direction and bring the arm back in a shallow curve as if preparing to place the bow on the string at the tip. Without interruption, the movement is then repeated a few times. This exercise is then repeated on imaginary down-bows, starting the recovery curve when the arm is fully extended and bringing the arm right back to the turning point well beyond the imaginary heel.

We then support the violin as shown in Diagrams 22 and 23 in this lesson, take up the bow and repeat the above up- and down-bow exercises several times on each string as follows:

In the up-bow version of this exercise, we should make sure that the whole arm follows through smoothly, which means that when the bow leaves the string at the heel, it simply takes off like an aeroplane and is not nervously snatched off. Although with the bow in the hand the right arm need not travel quite so far leftwards and upwards as it did when we performed this exercise without the bow, the return journey should not start until the back of the hand is about level with the nose.

At the turning point in the air, when the folded-up hand takes the full weight of the bow, one should be aware of a slight increase in tension, particularly in the little finger, a feeling similar to that experienced during the pressure-lift portion of the ricochet exercise. This 'coiled-spring' state of the hand is needed in order to cushion the shock of the touch-down in the down-bow version of this exercise. It will probably be necessary to experiment a certain amount with varying degrees of tension before arriving at a state in which the bow lands smoothly at the heel, giving a distinct start to the note, without scratch (excess tension) or splash (insufficient tension).

Two kinds of effort

There are two kinds of effort involved in bowing. One, which I call the 'smack-bounce', is a rapid thrust in one direction followed by a reaction in the opposite direction (like a ball bouncing off a wall). The other is a more prolonged and continuous effort in one direction only (like pushing or pulling a heavy load up a hill).

The first is essential to the change of direction (up-bow to down-bow and vice versa), the second occurs between changes of direction and corresponds to the sustained stroke proper.

None of the succeeding exercises require the violin, which can therefore be laid aside. When later the movements have been mastered, they should be practised again on the instrument, as illustrated in the diagrams. The scroll of the violin should, however, be supported as in the Preliminary Exercises with the Bow.

'Smack-bounce' exercises

The following exercises, practised at first without the bow, can be done in two directions, corresponding to the change from down-bow to up-bow and from up-bow to down-bow. They should be practised as if at both ends of the bow, and on the two extreme planes of the E string and G string with the hand in the appropriate playing position.

It is most natural to precede any throwing action in one direction by a slight preparatory movement in the opposite direction. In the following exercise you will begin with the hand in the neutral shape between the down- and the up-bow shape and prepare for the main throw by a quick small movement in the opposite direction.

QUICK UP-BOW, LONG DOWN-BOW

Make a quick upward movement of the wrist, together with a deliberate movement of the fingers into their bent position which brings the hand and fingers from an up-bow shape to a down-bow shape. This is immediately contradicted by the main pull of the arm in a down-bow stroke, together with the accompanying wrist movement.

When the forearm changes direction between the two strokes, the fingers and hand can continue the first stroke while the arm has already begun its movement in the opposite direction. Imagine that you have smacked your shoulder with the back of your hand.

45

This should be practised fairly quickly in two rhythms:

(a) ♪ ♪.   (b) ♪♪♪
3

The second bounce or third note in (b) is a reaction to the first one, only smaller and occurring naturally when allowed. In both versions all the joints should be as loose and flexible as possible, so that the whole movement resembles a whip-lash.

QUICK DOWN-BOW, LONG UP-BOW   ♪ ♪.

Here the main throw being away from the shoulder, all the actions described above are reversed and the smacking occurs, as it were, with the palm of the hand.

When the above exercises have been done enough times to capture the feeling, they should be tried with the bow, the fingers as loose as possible, until a sense of growing security replaces any fear you may have of dropping the bow.

So far the 'smack-bounces' have been done only in a straight line, but they can also be associated with the making of a circle or ellipse. The principle is the one of thrust and momentum used in the arm exercises in Lesson I (see pp. 26–7) with one impulse only to each circle. In this circle the smack is curved, and its impetus carries the hand, wrist and arm round the rest of the circle which is the re-bound.

Continuous effort (pull-push) exercises

In all the following exercises the bow is drawn across the first finger of the left hand, which simulates the friction of the bow hair on the strings. In playing, this friction will of course vary in proportion to the arm weight and finger pressure transferred to the strings through the bow.

The following will show in detail the adjustments necessary for keeping the bow absolutely parallel to the bridge, which depend on the flexibility of all the joints.

DOWN-BOW

We start from the folded position at the heel (Diagram 24). The upper arm and shoulder-blade falling back pull the passive forearm with them. The elbow angle remains almost constant until the middle of the bow is approached, when the forearm begins to lead. The wrist is gradually lowered.

In the middle of the bow (Diagram 25) the back of the hand, the wrist and the forearm are approximately in a straight line.

In the upper half of the bow (Diagram 26) the forearm leads, pulling the upper arm forward. As the whole arm straightens, the elbow is rotated slightly upwards (a movement which is initiated in the upper arm), and the wrist begins to fall below the straight line. The shoulder in rotation is pulled forward right from the shoulder-blade, as if reaching over the bow stroke. The wrist takes over from the forearm in the last part of the stroke, pulling the hand, and reaching its lowest point at the tip. Finally, at the very end of the stroke, the fingers begin going into the up-bow position.

Diagram 24
Lower half of bow

Diagram 25
Middle of bow

Diagram 26
Upper half of bow

Diagram 27
Upper half of bow

Diagram 28
Middle of bow

Diagram 29
Lower half of bow

UP-BOW

We start from the extended position at the tip (Diagram 27), and to begin the up-bow, the wrist rises slightly. The forearm then leads, pushing the upper arm together with the shoulder and shoulder-blade back and down. The back relaxes and feels as if it is expanding sideways throughout the whole course of the up-bow. The forearm also rotates slightly outwards from the elbow.

In the middle of the bow (Diagram 28) the back of the hand, the wrist and forearm are approximately in a straight line.

In the lower half of the bow (Diagram 29) the upper arm provides the driving power. This motive force must flow unbroken right into the bow, despite the changing configuration of the wrist and fingers. (If an actual acute angle is formed at the wrist joint, this flow is interrupted.) In the very last part of the stroke, before the following down-bow, the fingers prepare the down-bow by following through into the down-bow shape. The movement of the shoulder-blade, which in fact begins at the start of the up-bow but becomes more pronounced in the lower half, is felt as a 'rightwards-spreading'. At the same time one should have a distinct sense of its function in counter-balancing the weight of the rising upper arm and forearm.

Finger and thumb movements

In both the 'smack-bounce' and the continuous pull-push, you must remember to apply the various opposing movements of the thumb and fingers discussed on page 37 (combination of 'circle' and 'bridge').

To get a greater feeling of the bow-hair's grip on the finger (string), whether very slight or firm, the opposing pressures in the 'bridge' can be used in a new way. We have seen how the piers spread away from each other in both the down- and the up-bow. In the down-bow the first finger will pull towards you, while the fourth finger pushes away against the inside of the stick (Diagram 30).

In the up-bow the play is between the first and third fingers, the latter pulling towards you, as illustrated in Diagram 31.

Diagram 30

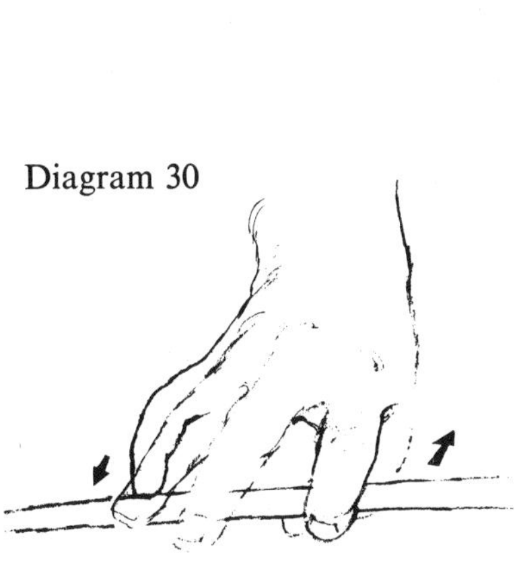

Diagram 31

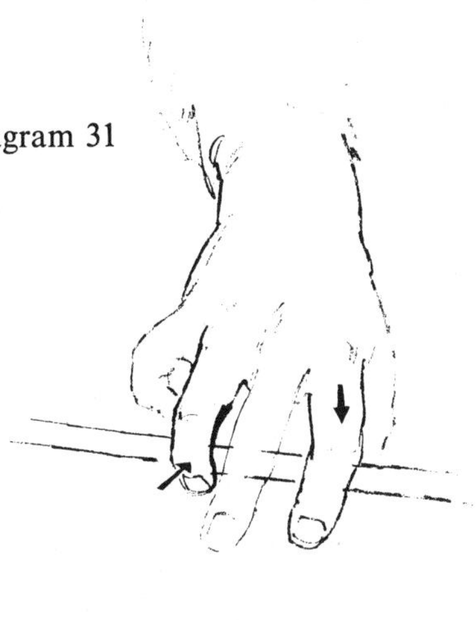

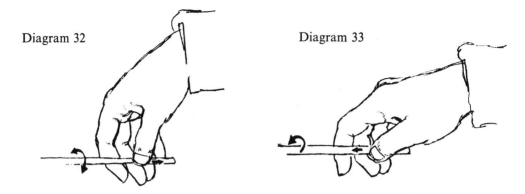

Diagram 32   Diagram 33

It is necessary to provide a counter-pressure to the string to prevent the bow actually sliding towards you or away from you on the string, and this counter-pressure is another function of the roll of the bow already mentioned in connection with the 'circle' formed by the thumb and second finger (Diagrams 32 and 33).

Rest the bow-hair on the first finger of the left hand and, as described above for the down-bow, pull in with the first finger and push away with the fourth so that the stick moves towards you – without, however, disturbing the bow-hair which remains in place and flat on the finger. The stick is righted by an upward roll of the thumb against the second finger.

In the up-bow the stick, this time pushed away from you by the action of the first and third fingers as illustrated above, is righted by the downward roll of the thumb against the second finger.

I must point out that though we have thought of the pull and push as continuing along the whole bow length, it is often necessary to be able to feel it in a very short stroke. Conversely, though the 'smack-bounce' is normally a small movement involving a short length of bow, it can also be used to travel its whole length. We will return to these in Lesson IV.

Combination of continuous pull-push and 'smack-bounce'

When you have accustomed yourself to the continuous pull and push of the down- and up-bows you should be able to link them together with a 'smack-bounce' movement at each change of bow.

Starting in the folded position, for example, we pull-smack-bounce, push-smack-bounce, pull-smack-bounce, etc. An easy way to get this feeling is to think of a figure 8, although only a trace of the figure will remain in most playing situations.

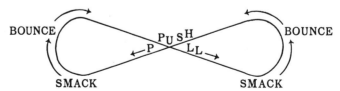

BOUNCE   BOUNCE

PUSH
PULL

SMACK   SMACK

The musical effect of this movement is the rhythmic pattern:

Return to minimum effort and basic bow hold

For some time now we have been concentrating on elements of strength and speed and many small details of finger pressures in thrust and momentum, but we should often return to the opposite as an antidote – to the floating state of minimum effort, the starting point or 'zero' state, in which the bow is supported by the right hand alone.

In this state we can more easily become aware of the general responsibilities of the hand in balancing the bow, and the upper arm and shoulder in carrying its weight along a stroke in the air.

Remember too that there is one main bow hold to which we shall always return, as described at the beginning of this lesson. Here, the thumb is always rounded (bent) with its joint pointing towards the tip of the bow – whether, as in the down-bow, the thumb rolls the stick clockwise or, as in the up-bow anti-clockwise, its general position is always pressed against the stick. All other movements associated with up- or down-bow directions are subsidiary to this principal hold. When we have developed this great flexibility, we must beware against exaggerating these movements. In effect they will become almost invisible. They will be felt from within, particularly those associated with the right-hand fingers. It must be remembered that the right-hand fingers almost never originate motion. Rather do they carry and transmit the impulses from the bigger joints behind them.

We use these exercises to develop flexibility and co-ordination, but after a thousand exercises we must finally forget the 'grammar' with all its exceptions and counter-rules and return to this basic, flexible, resilient but least agitated hold.

Of course, in violin playing not only the two extremes are needed (carrying the bow in the air or applying full strength on the string) but the infinite degrees between them. To enable the violinist to respond to any demands, expressive or technical, which music may make, the violinist must not only control this whole range, but be able at will to change constantly from one extreme to the other in any circumstance.

We will conclude this lesson with another series of continuous full bow strokes, both fast and slow, but this time without the support and assistance of the left hand, taking care that the right hand is as soft as possible without losing the bow. Remember that the characteristic sound of the violin is an expressive melodic one, a legato line drawn forth by this continuous movement of the bow which can give the illusion of one continuous sound.

LESSON III

Preparatory Exercises – Left Hand

Common faults in holding the violin

We speak of holding the violin, but the word 'hold', with its implication of a firm and static grip, can be misleading. We should remember that the violinist, unlike the pianist or cellist, whose instruments rest on the floor, must support his instrument unaided (nor can the violinist hide or take shelter behind or beneath his instrument!). Furthermore, this support has to be achieved in such a way as to incorporate at any time the freest possible motion over the whole fingerboard; and moreover this motion has to be co-ordinated with every conceivable movement of the right hand. Here, as with the bow, the development of a sense of balance and flexibility will form a far freer and healthier basis on which later to apply strength and effort, than would clamping the violin between the shoulder and head, or clutching it between the thumb and first finger of the left hand.

The basic difference in the use of the thumb on the violin and on the piano is that the violinist has perforce to support his instrument and hold the bow, and he has to learn how to relax the thumb between every effort. (After all, the pianist does not have to support his piano.) It is very important to let go of the hold, since the grasping of the thumb against fingers prevents the freedom of our movements.

With the piano, the thumb is treated as another finger, and is always relaxed when it is not playing – when it is not putting down a note – which makes piano playing so much more easy. Until we learn to relax and develop the thumb, we will not do our best with violin playing; hence my great stress on the thumb and on learning to use it.

The hold

There are only two sources of support necessary for the violin: one passive – the collarbone – which is relatively fixed (the violin is moved on the collarbone); the other active – the left hand – which is constantly mobile or ready to move (the hand moves the violin). The light pressure (weight) of the head on the chin-rest prevents the violin from slipping off the shelf of the collarbone.

The point of the shoulder – where the arm joins the body – is thus relieved of any responsibility to support the violin and should be allowed to remain in a normal relaxed position. This means that the violinist is free to retain a relaxed posture while holding or playing his instrument, and it eliminates the hunching of the left shoulder common to many violinists, which is not only a frequent source of considerable discomfort and pain but also impedes free movement, whether large or small, of the arm and fingers.

It is preferable to do without a shoulder-pad or a shoulder-rest. If used as a support,

52

the shoulder is restricted in its freedom of movement, and if actively 'clamped', the shoulder is 'frozen'. For those with a long neck and an unpronounced collarbone a shoulder-rest or a folded cloth can be a great comfort, but under no conditions should it be more than gently touched – *without* pressure.

In order to hold the violin as I shall describe, it is useful to have a chin-rest with a fairly prominent lip. The Carl Flesch model is a good design, but chin-rests are largely a matter of personal choice.

Diagram 1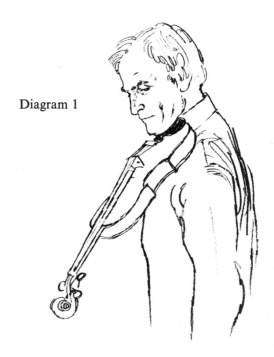

Learning to support the violin

HEAD AND COLLARBONE SUPPORT

Start with the violin hanging from the hold between the head and collarbone (as in Diagram 1); both the arms should be hanging loosely at your sides. The violin will slope downwards, pointing towards the floor, and is prevented from slipping away by the weight of the head and a backwards pull of the chin on the chin-rest. Naturally, more effort with the head is needed until the left hand takes its share of the weight, but this head action (the 'pull' part of the chicken-like push and pull of the head introduced in Lesson I, p. 21) will be very important in descending shifts. The violin, even when hanging, does not actually touch the shoulder, which should be completely relaxed and free to move independently of the violin.

53

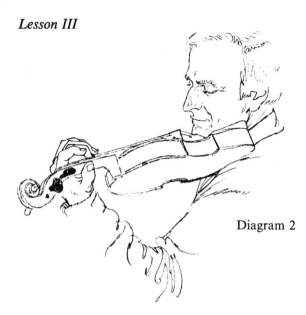

Diagram 2

Now place the pad of the left thumb on the side of the instrument's neck and the second finger on the A string half-way along the neck. The head, its backward pull no longer needed for support, now rests lightly on the chin-rest, just touching enough to prevent the violin slipping off the collarbone. Now raise the violin to a position approximately parallel to the floor (if anything, a little higher) adjusting the head to the violin's new angle by lifting the head momentarily above the chin-rest and replacing it afresh. The shoulder should remain hanging freely, so there is now the maximum space between it and the violin.

This exercise is especially useful for acquiring the feeling of the hold between the head and collarbone.

LEFT-HAND SUPPORT (at first without the violin)
Now we shall concentrate on the left-hand support. We shall begin by supporting the whole weight of the left arm with the right hand (its thumb in the left palm), which should be opposite the left shoulder, about a foot away from it, and approximately at shoulder level. The arm should be hanging absolutely loosely and can be swung like a pendulum. The wrist should be in a straight line with the hand and arm. Now gradually allow the left arm to support itself with the minimum of effort, without disturbing the natural hanging position of the elbow which is the basic one from which we shall work. The fingers and thumb should be soft and rounded.

Diagram 3

Diagram 4

THUMB EXERCISE

Using the first finger of the right hand as a substitute for the violin, place it on the pad of the left thumb, pushing the top thumb phalange a little to the left until it is quite vertical. You will notice that the pad of the thumb is now diagonal. This means that when we press the first finger gently down, it can gather the flesh of the pad into a cushion of support. Keeping the contact, alternately apply and release the pressure – the thumb should return to its original straighter position with the release, though its top phalange should automatically remain vertical. This suppleness of the thumb is the key both to left-hand support and flexibility, and to the angle and height of the knuckles.

You should now be ready to return to the violin with a variant of the first exercise in holding the instrument, this time focusing your attention on the left-hand support.

The violin, held between the head and collarbone, is now supported at the scroll by someone else or by leaning it gently against a smooth wall. As in the first exercise, let both arms hang loosely at your sides and then bring the left hand up to playing position without disturbing the softness of the arm or the hanging position of the shoulder. In fact, when the arm is lifted away from the side, the shoulder, tipped back by the upper arm becoming more parallel to the floor, drops further still. I would like you to be aware of this tendency now, although its importance will only become more apparent when we begin to move in our hold. The head should rest lightly on the chin-rest.

Diagram 6

Diagram 5

Diagram 7

Very gradually allow the external support of the violin to be replaced by your own left thumb, the weight of the violin making its own supporting cushion on the thumb's pad, as the right-hand first finger did previously (see Diagram 5). The top phalange of the thumb is now almost, but not quite, vertical. Once this rather delicate balance has been caught, you will find that any downward pressure on the fingerboard, far from making the violin slip, will only serve to increase its security, based as it is on friction. Violinists with 'double-jointed' thumbs who find this difficult should persevere, as it provides a means of overcoming this handicap.

General description of the hold

I have already mentioned that the fingers should be soft and rounded, the elbow hanging and the wrist straight, and I have stressed the importance of the flexibility and security of the thumb support. We now must bring the fingers over the strings by slightly rotating the forearm (with the sympathetic adjustment of the hanging elbow) until the knuckles are at an angle almost parallel to the fingerboard. Try this movement, noticing that as the fingers (which should still be soft and curved) are brought over the strings they separate, and a circular shape is formed between the thumb and each finger as in the right hand on the bow. To achieve this shape it is necessary, with the slight rotation of the forearm, for the base joint of the first finger to come away from the neck and that of the fourth finger to come closer to the neck without disturbing the shape and contact of the thumb. Only then will all the fingers, even the shorter fourth one, be rounded and in constant readiness to cross the fingerboard to any string with a minimum of adjustment to the general position. This is the 'golden-mean' position which should be so perfectly balanced and so effortless as to allow an equal range of movement in all directions (Diagrams 6 and 7).

To be able to travel up and down the fingerboard past the shoulder of the violin with a similar minimum of adjustment, the knuckles must be at a height which allows an uninterrupted movement to the highest position. The following group of exercises, depending on the mobility of the thumb and the softness of all its joints, especially the base joint, will help you to achieve these ideals.

Exercises for movement in the hold, especially thumb flexibility

The normal playing position of the thumb is the bent one and, of course, the more bent it is, the higher in relation to the fingerboard the knuckles will automatically be. You must be aware that this bend is not due to a conscious effort, but to the softness of the thumb which allows the weight of the violin to push it down (as the right-hand first finger did in the earlier exercise).

First, two exercises in the *lateral direction*.

EXERCISE 1

Hold the violin this way with the fingers over the fingerboard but not touching the strings. Now move only the top phalange of the thumb from side to side, keeping the arm, wrist, hand and lower part of the thumb motionless but soft. The violin moves

57

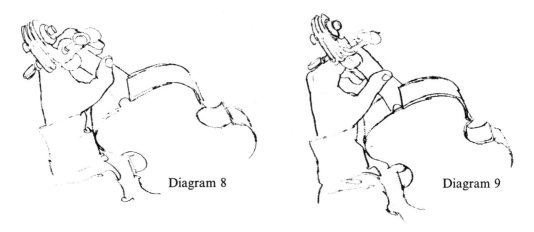

Diagram 8

Diagram 9

from side to side with the thumb. This change of angle of the top phalange of the thumb will be used in shifting.

EXERCISE 2

Here is a more difficult variation which you can try now but which will become easier only after later exercises. Beginning in the same position, place a finger, say the second, on any string, and lift the head off the chin-rest. Now rock the violin itself with the finger and thumb, to the right by the finger pulling while the thumb becomes more bent, to the left by the finger pushing as the thumb straightens.

Now two exercises in the *vertical direction:* the first moving the arm like a pendulum, keeping the violin still; the second moving the violin, keeping the arm still.

EXERCISE 3

Begin as in Exercise 1, the hand in its highest position, thumb bent. Swing the elbow far enough to the left to bring the lower phalange of the thumb into a straight line with the top one, almost perpendicular to the floor – this movement also brings the

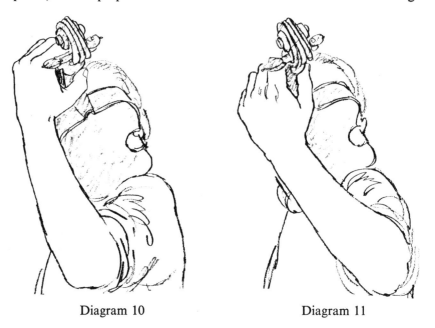

Diagram 10

Diagram 11

58

fingers away from the fingerboard and the knuckles lower in relation to it. Then swing the elbow back to its original position. The thumb, by bending, allows this movement to lift the knuckles back into their highest position in relation to the fingerboard. Repeat this swinging movement several times, taking care that the top phalange of the thumb remains virtually motionless. This exercise is the opposite of Exercise 1 in which this phalange only moved, while the rest of the thumb and arm were still. Here again, the principle of working from a height is helpful as the change of position and vibrato are helped by lightness in the hand.

EXERCISE 4
Again, begin as before, but this time, instead of the elbow-swing bringing the thumb into a straight line, the elbow remains in its normal hanging position, and the thumb itself pushes up until it is straight, lifting the violin with it, so that the knuckles are now in their lowest position in relation to the fingerboard, although they themselves have not actually moved. Now relax the thumb so that the weight of the violin pushes it back to its bent position. This exercise is complementary to Exercise 3, the straightening of the thumb here being achieved by its own effort instead of by the swing of the arm. But the main point of the exercise is the release, not the straightening of the thumb. Although the top phalange moves up and down, its angle remains unchanged, as in Exercise 3.

Addition of fingers – their movement and flexibility

Now we shall do the last two exercises again, but this time with the addition of each finger in turn. It is important to do every exercise on each string (beginning with the A and ending with the G string) in at least three different parts of the fingerboard – roughly below, at and above the shoulder of the violin. The easiest finger to begin with in all the exercises is the second, which should then be followed by the third, fourth and first fingers in that order. It is especially important to work on the fourth finger in all the exercises right from the beginning.

You remember that the arm rotation which brings the fingers over the fingerboard naturally tends to separate them from each other without introducing tension. This is important, as the fingers should never lean on one another, because it is their very separation which will enable each one to work independently of the others. It is therefore essential to keep the same angle of the knuckles (almost parallel to the fingerboard) while working with the first finger as with the fourth. In other words, the slight forearm rotation should become an unconscious habit throughout all exercises and playing, counteracting any inclination of the hand and fingers to fall away from the fingerboard when the fourth finger is not being used. This rotation occurs naturally with each elbow-swing, or 'pendel' as I like to call it, to the right.

EXERCISE 3 REPEATED
Place the second finger lightly on the A string on a harmonic (that is, not pressing the string down) a little above the thumb so that the thumb is opposite the first finger (its usual position); the string should cross the soft pad of the finger-tip diagonally.

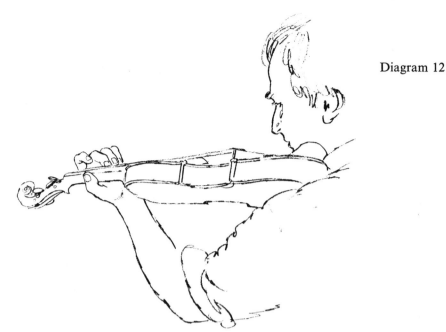

Diagram 12

As the thumb is bent, the knuckles are in their highest position, and thus the second finger, though not actually vertical, is at its steepest angle to the fingerboard. In this position we find and create the greatest space – space between the fingers, space in the circle between the thumb and second finger (or whichever finger is on the string) and therefore space between the neck of the violin and the base knuckle of the first finger, and – fundamental to the later exercises and my whole approach – the maximum space between the shoulder and the violin.

In holding the violin, the more flexible the left thumb joint, the more naturally the left elbow will swing to the right and up. It is very important to bear in mind this flexibility of the left thumb.

Continuing as in Exercise 3, swing the elbow to the left.
Like the top phalange of the thumb, the top phalange of the second finger should remain at a constant angle to the fingerboard.
As the two phalanges of the thumb are brought into a straight line by the elbow-swing, which simultaneously lowers the knuckles, the second-finger joints will bend. When the elbow

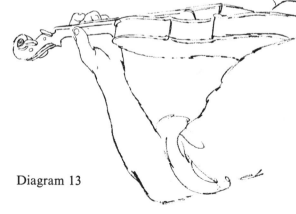

Diagram 13

60

swings back and up to the right, the thumb will bend and the finger straighten. Although the wrist should be soft, it should remain in a straight line with the forearm and back of the hand – up to the base knuckles in the high position, and up to the second joint knuckles in the low position; everything thus depends on the suppleness of the base joint of the thumb. The main effect of the elbow-swing is to move the fingers over the different strings.

Co-ordination with shoulder and arm movements

In all violin playing the shoulder should be free to react to every movement of the arm: in this case, there is a similarity to a see-saw action in that when the elbow-swing to the right lifts the hand into a high position the shoulder falls, and when the elbow-swing to the left pulls the hand into a low position, the shoulder returns to its slightly higher position (which is nevertheless a relaxed one). When the shoulder is allowed to react naturally, the movement will be quite small – there should be no effort or exaggeration. The higher the violin, the lower the shoulder. I have deliberately connected the free elbow-swing to the right with the throwing of the hand away and up, in other words, with a protruding left wrist (see Diagram 14); and the swing to the left with an ingoing wrist and the throwing of the hand, as it were, towards the player's body or towards the bridge of the violin (see Diagram 15). This

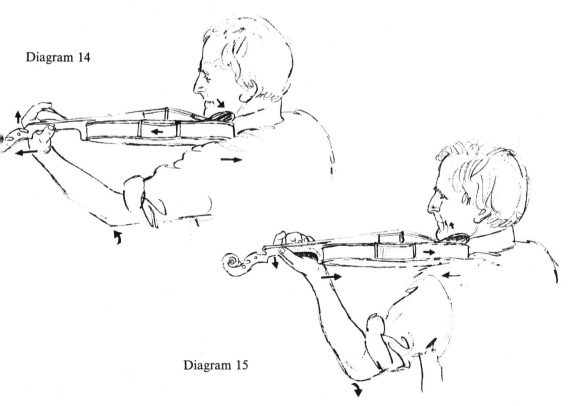

Diagram 14

Diagram 15

is the oscillating movement that leads directly to the vibrato. It does not cover a long distance on the fingerboard, because it is more of a pivot movement (Diagram 16) than a long-distance carrying movement. This is easily understood by noting that as the elbow moves in one direction, the hand moves the opposite way; as the elbow swings left, the hand is swung in the direction of the bridge, and vice versa.

I have concentrated on this basic reflex becauses it enhances the balanced stance and the balanced hand on the violin. But it is necessary to stress, already at this point, that it is perfectly possible to initiate the hand movement towards the bridge with a free elbow-swing to the right, shown in exaggerated form in Diagram 17, which goes again into the wrist, throwing the hand forward; and by the same token, it is perfectly possible with a lower swing to the left to throw the hand backwards towards the scroll of the violin. The application of these two complementary movements depends on the direction and momentum of the right hand. Thus, in a down-bow it is more natural to shift to a higher position, i.e. towards the bridge, with an elbow-swing to the right (see Diagram 17). In an up-bow, however, it is more natural to initiate this shift with the elbow pivoting to the left (see Diagram 16).

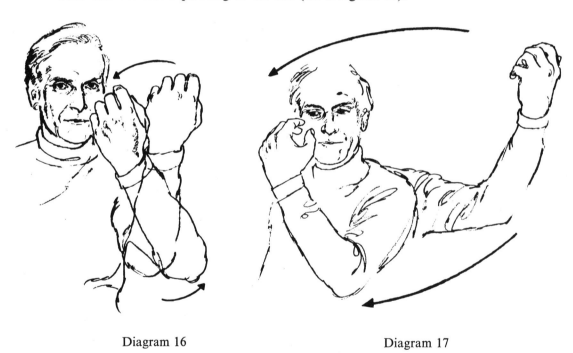

Diagram 16   Diagram 17

EXERCISE 4 REPEATED

This exercise will help you to co-ordinate the different movements of the thumb and fingers, and further develop the suppleness of the thumb.

Begin with one finger on a harmonic. Without disturbing the hand or the hanging position of the arm, raise and lower the violin only with the thumb, which pushes upwards and is then released into its bent position. When the thumb straightens, the finger bends, and vice versa, the top phalange of both thumb and finger remaining at a constant angle to the finger-board.

Exercise in lifting the fingers

Place all the fingers lightly as for harmonics on one string. Each finger should be rounded and soft and separated from its neighbours. Without disturbing the three remaining fingers, each finger in turn should be lifted as high and as rapidly as possible up into the air, sometimes straight, more often retaining its rounded shape, and then allowed to fall gently back on to its harmonic. The movement should be repeated several times, care being taken not to tighten the hand (Diagrams 18 and 19).

This should be practised at first with consecutive fingers, then in any order, and then with more than one finger at a time. It should also be practised on each string, and finally with the fingers each on a different string. Remember that it is as important in violin playing to concentrate on the lift of the fingers as on their fall. When it comes to actual performance, there are good physiological grounds for restricting the lifting of the fingers to the minimum consistent with clarity.

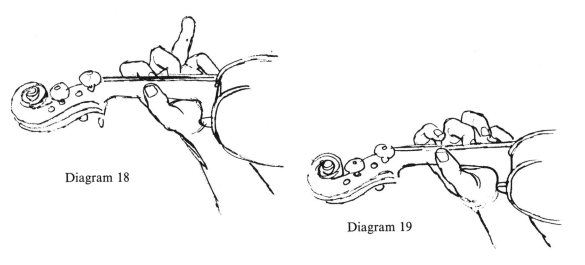

Diagram 18

Diagram 19

Pressure

In violin playing one must be careful not to associate the word 'pressure' with contraction any more than one associates the word 'hold' with grip. If we place the finger-tips of one hand against the finger-tips of the other, we can apply pressure in two ways. One way is a squeeze of the arms which closes in on the space contracting it; the other way is an expanding of the whole circle formed by hands, arms, shoulders and back. We make the circle bigger the more we press the finger-tips against each other. This principle applies to all opposition, including finger v. thumb, etc.

In the left hand the movement and feeling are as follows. Hold the violin with the hand in its usual high position, with the second finger on a harmonic on the A string. First, to discover how much (or how little) effort is needed to stop the string, gradually apply enough pressure to bring it into contact with the fingerboard. It is most important that the angle of the finger is such that the pad of the finger touches the fingerboard equally on both sides of the string. As you alternate between this gentle pressure and its release to the harmonic, the feeling of expansion inside the hand-shape during the pressure comes from a slight further lift of the knuckles which should occur simultaneously with, or, more accurately, as a result of, the pushing down of the finger. This slight lift is accompanied by the appropriate reaction in the arm and shoulder, the elbow moving a little to the right, and the shoulder falling back, both resembling a miniature version of the see-saw action mentioned on p. 61. The opposite happens in the release. The pressure of the finger on the string must be applied in an absolutely vertical direction so that the string is never pushed or pulled to one side.

This exercise, having first been done with the finger returning to the harmonic on each release, should now be practised taking the finger right off the string on the release. As your finger touches the string again, let it be sensitive to the harmonic through which it passes before you apply pressure. It is important in all the exercises that the fingers not in use should remain soft and separated from each other, and *not* be allowed to lean on the active finger. They should remain above and close to the string and all at approximately the same level.

After working with each finger separately, you should try alternating between any pair of adjacent fingers, and eventually between any fingers in any order. There are two ways in which this can be practised:

(a) When the finger which first applies pressure releases to the harmonic, the next finger is simultaneously placed on a harmonic. When the latter finger applies its pressure downwards, the first is simultaneously lifted upwards. Therefore, both fingers arrive at and leave their harmonics simultaneously but from opposite directions.

(b) This time, the finger which first applies pressure is taken right off the string in its release before the next finger approaches the string.

The main difference between these two exercises is that between each application of pressure both fingers rest on a harmonic in the first, but in the air in the second. However, common to both and most important is the complete relaxation of all effort between each pressure – one of the main principles in playing mentioned at the beginning of this lesson.

Be sure that you remember the reactions of the hand, arm and shoulder which should accompany each application of pressure. Take care that the angle of the top finger phalange to the fingerboard is not altered by the rising of the knuckles and that the finger-tip is in contact with the fingerboard equally on both sides of the string; each of these points ensure that the string is neither pushed nor pulled to one side.

Horizontal movement

So far we have concentrated on the vertical movement of the hands and fingers which, through the softness of the thumb's base joint, gives us the required height of the knuckles over the fingerboard. Now we shall learn the horizontal movements which are the basis for vibrato and for the impetus needed to travel up and down the fingerboard.

In this exercise, and in many yet to come, we are working from a middle position, passing through it as we go from one extreme to the other. You must remember that when we play, we will never stay in the middle position and we will rarely touch the extremes, but as a result of working at them we will have more control over, and more flexibility and strength in all the degrees between.

Begin with one finger pressing a string down about half-way up the fingerboard (to avoid hitting pegs), the knuckles in their usual high position, fingers separated. Keeping the finger-tip anchored in one place, pull the wrist away from you and out of its usual straight line so that it pulls the knuckles backwards. This pull away should be combined with a slight upward thrust of the knuckles accompanied by an elbow-swing to the right, and the shoulder should react in the opposite direction, away from the knuckles (Diagram 20).

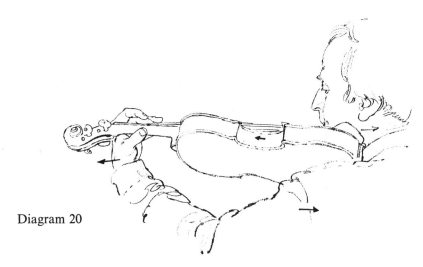

Diagram 20

This movement of the wrist, in pulling the knuckles backwards towards the head of the violin, gradually straightens the thumb and the finger which is on the string, altering the angle of the finger to the fingerboard. The other fingers, which remain in the air, will also be lengthened and should touch each other as little as is consistent with their remaining soft. Because you are pulling the violin away from the hold between the collarbone and the head, the latter must simultaneously pull back on the chin-rest, but only enough to prevent the violin slipping.

65

Lesson III

After holding the extreme position for a moment, release the pull so that you return to the normal soft position in which you began, knuckles still high, thumb bent, head resting lightly on the chin-rest. This movement should be practised several times before going on to the next, which in its turn should be repeated.

Now, from this position go to the other extreme, the wrist pushing the knuckles in towards you so that this time the finger on the string bends to its most folded position, but the thumb once again becomes straighter. The knuckles are lowered, the elbow swings to the left and the shoulder again reacts in the opposite direction to the

Diagram 21

knuckles, this time towards them. Like the finger which is pressing on the string, the other fingers will bend, remaining soft and separated. Now that you are pushing the violin into your neck, even the light resting of the head on the chin-rest is no longer needed to prevent the violin slipping. Although in playing the head normally touches the chin-rest all the time, one should be very aware of the three different sensations of pulling back, resting lightly, and having no responsibility at all. In this exercise one should actually raise the head off the chin-rest, but only far enough just to lose contact. Having held this extreme position for a moment, as in the outward direction, release the push, returning again to the normal position ready to repeat the whole cycle.

To make sure that these alternating sensations and their co-ordination are correct, substitute your right hand for the violin, the left thumb in the right palm, the second finger on the back of the right hand. You now have a clear view of the shoulder and arm, and can check all the movements visually as you push and pull against your right hand, always pausing briefly in the middle position.

66

While you are still in this position, the right hand taking the place of the violin, here is a variant which will enable you to become aware of a tendency of the thumb to push in contrary motion to the finger and the direction of the knuckles, the importance of which will be enlarged on later. Do the above exercise, but now keep the wrist in more of a straight line with the back of the hand and forearm, and make a brisk movement from one extreme to the other, altogether eliminating any pause in the middle position. Throughout the exercise remember the previously mentioned upward thrust which should always be associated with the extension of the knuckles as they move away from you. This raising of the knuckles is fundamental in downward shifts, and should become a habit. Having done this several times, let the finger slide back and forth a little on the right hand, the knuckles pulling it back to its most extended position when the elbow moves to the right, and the knuckles pushing it forward into its most folded position when the elbow moves to the left. Though the thumb always remains on the same point, acting as a pivot, you will soon be able to feel that it is by no means passive, as it aids the thrust of the knuckles by pushing towards you when the knuckles are extended away from you (finger straight) and pushing away from you when the knuckles push in towards you (finger bent).

I am not concentrating on the other pair of movements (i.e. moving towards the bridge with the elbow-swing to the right, and the movement towards the violin head with the elbow-swing to the left). These are relatively easy and do not, in training, contribute to the mastery of a balanced hold of the violin, which demands rather an elbow trained to swing to the right as the hand is thrust up and away from the body.

Circles

We have practised separately the vertical, horizontal and lateral movements, all of which involve the natural swing of the elbow. These three directions, each involving a pair of extremes (vertical pair – up and down; horizontal pair – away from and towards you; lateral pair – right and left), should now be co-ordinated on the violin so as to produce a circle traced by the knuckles, which involves the flexible movement of all the finger and thumb joints, the wrist, and the elbow. The knuckles either rise from the far side of the circle and come towards you over the top, or rise on the near side of the circle and go away from you over the top. The object of all our efforts is to avoid head-on collisions between movements and to ensure their harmonious integration.

Opposition of thumb to knuckles and finger – 3 exercises

1. The thumb stays on one point, the finger slides.
2. The finger-tip stays on one point, the thumb slides.
3. The thumb and finger slide simultaneously in contrary motion.

EXERCISE 1
Begin as before with the second finger pressing the string down about half-way up

Diagram 22

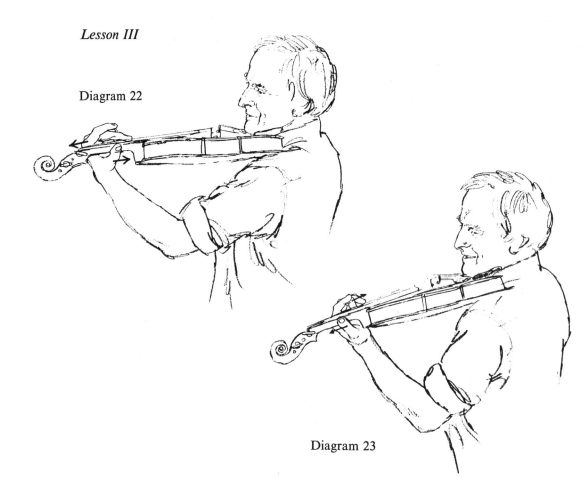

Diagram 23

the fingerboard. Now push the knuckles back, simultaneously pushing forward with the thumb (Diagram 22). The thumb as a stationary but active pivot helps the knuckles to extend the finger (which lengthens towards the scroll) and also assists the elbow in its swing to the right. Return to the middle position and still pivoting on the thumb, push the knuckles forward. This time the thumb pushes away from you, the finger becomes folded and slides up the string towards the head, and the elbow swings to the left (Diagram 23). In both these movements the shoulder reacts in the opposite direction to the knuckles, as usual. (You must also remember the lift of the knuckles when you pull them away from you.)

When you are accustomed to these movements, you can eliminate the pauses in the middle position and move briskly from one extreme to the other. Then try the exercise with other fingers.

EXERCISE 2

In this exercise the finger-tip remains on one point while the thumb actually slides in the direction of its push. Otherwise all the reactions detailed in Exercise 1 remain the same.

EXERCISE 3

This exercise is a combination of Exercises 1 and 2. The finger-tip and the thumb now slide in contrary motion. The distance they travel should be quite short, otherwise it will be difficult to pull back and lift the knuckles in the opposite direction to the thumb's forward push.

Plucking (pizzicato) with the left hand

This is a good exercise for finger flexibility, as even in plucking the fingers should not be rigid.

Place the second finger lightly on the D string in its normal position, keeping the other fingers soft and separated in the air over the fingerboard. Press the string down, at the same time pulling it in such a way that the top joint of the finger gives way.

Diagram 24

As always when the finger applies pressure, the expansion in the knuckles and hand should result in the co-operative movement, however slight, of the whole arm and shoulder (see-saw action, p. 61) which must be in a 'floating state' ready to respond and adjust even to the most microscopic finger movements.

The finger, continuing its sideways pull, releases the string, and its top joint, always soft and elastic, springs back to its normal bent position. This exercise should be done with each finger on all the strings.

Further plucking exercises

1. (a) In first position, place the first finger on A on the G string, the second on F♯ on the D string, the third on D on the A string, and the fourth on B on the E string. Pluck several times with each finger in turn, the other fingers resting softly and curved on their notes (at first on harmonics, later pressing down). Do not forget the slight raising of the knuckles with each plucking movement.

(b) The same movement as in (a) but this time the first finger is on F on the E string, the second on C on the A string, the third on G on the D string, and the fourth on D on the G string. This is a more difficult position, calling for a slight elbow-swing to the right in addition to the usual high position of the knuckles. This

69

will enable the shorter fourth finger to be brought over the G string without losing its curved shape. You must be careful not to let the first and second fingers pull the E and A strings.

2. (a) Place all the fingers on the E string and then pluck the A, D and G strings with each finger in turn, taking care not to disturb the three fingers remaining on the E string.

(b) Now place the fingers on the G string and pluck the D, A and E strings with each finger in turn.

Sliding with each finger

This movement is necessary in chromatic melodic passages, and in double-stopping.

Begin with all four fingers on one string, leaving a space between each finger-tip. With each finger in turn, slide as far up and down an adjacent string as permitted by the other fingers which remain anchored. This can be done in two ways – either by involving the active and visible co-operation not only of the fingers and the knuckles but also of the whole arm, or by isolating the independent movement of the sliding finger while keeping the hand and arm soft.

The same exercise should be done with two fingers simultaneously sliding in opposite directions. In this case, the effort is concentrated in the hand and fingers, as in the second way above.

Independence of the fingers

There is an extremely valuable series of exercises by D. C. Dounis which combine simultaneous movements of lifting, plucking with, and sliding the fingers. They are called *The Complete Independence of 3 Fingers*, and *The Complete Independence of 4 Fingers*, published by Lavender Publications and available through Novello & Co., Ltd., London. These can already be practised at this stage, though you will not yet be able to do them with the bow as they are intended to be done.

LESSON IV

Bow Movements

It is impossible to describe in detail the innumerable inflections of finger and joint movements in all their staggering complexity, and furthermore it is unnecessary. I feel it is sufficient to recognize the main movements so that, during performance, they become available to the violinist in all their myriad applications.

Some very gifted players, already highly talented at a tender age, are inspired and are physically uninhibited and pliable enough to co-ordinate their movements. They may never know impediments. This state of grace, however, does not necessarily survive the age of questioning and the trials of life, unless a firm foundation has been laid and unless some conscious guide-lines have been provided, and – let it be said again – unless music has retained for the individual its meaning and its demanding hold on the ear and the imagination of the player.

At this point, you should review Lesson II where a detailed account was given of the basic bow hold, as well as of the adjustments necessary to keep the bow parallel to the bridge. Then, as an essential preliminary to the exercises which follow, let us first consider the three sections of a completed down-bow stroke.

Basic bow stroke

A. INITIAL IMPULSE
The right upper arm pulls and carries; in effect this produces an anti-clockwise rotation of the upper arm. This part of the stroke can be isolated as one short sound *sf*; it can occur at any part of the bow or for any fraction of its length, even for the whole length of a fast stroke, and may be loud or soft.

B. SUSTAINED SECTION
The sustained portion of the stroke requires a firmer hold (strengthening of piers) and a feeling of the resistance of the string. The arm, wrist and fingers function as a single, articulated unit throughout this section, which may cover any length of the bow and may be slow or fast, loud or soft.

C. CONNECTING SECTION
In the final section the stroke is absorbed into the wrist, which is now relaxed, and the hand assumes the shape of the up-bow beginning. This third part of the stroke already belongs to the up-bow stroke. This section, too, can be anything from a minute and almost imperceptible change of bow between strokes to a fairly substantial fast stroke as in vigorous dotted rhythms. (In up-bows the hand, of course, assumes the shape of the down-bow beginning.)

A stroke, whether fast or slow, long or short, loud or soft, can use A, B and C together in equal proportions; it can also be predominantly any one of these. When doing down- and up-bows almost exclusively with B's, the fingers are almost still and there is no momentum or 'throw'. The forearm (or when at the heel, the elbow) covers the same distance as the bow on the string.

In working on the right-hand positions in down- and up-bows, it will be found that the raising of the knuckles in the up-bow also involves an altering of the knuckle angle so that they point slightly more in the direction of the up-bow. This must happen as a consequence of the lengthening of the fingers – particularly of the second and third fingers – and as a result of exercises developing a balanced hold of the bow between first and second (also first, second and third) fingers and thumb. Try to play with one finger at a time on the bow, to discover for yourself the function of each, and try to feel distinctly the independence and difference of function between the first and second fingers. The first finger has a distinct lateral action in its base (knuckle) joint which demands a special awareness and a softness independent of the second finger action.

The action described above will facilitate, lighten and speed the bow strokes, enabling the player to use a stroke composed only of sections A and C (by-passing B) of the Basic Stroke. This stroke resolves itself into a single impulse stroke, either staccato in short bows, or a fast, light, smooth and soft détaché in longer bows, even whole bows.

Exercises on the basic bow stroke

EXERCISE 1

Hold the violin in the playing position, the third finger on the note D on a harmonic in the first position on the A string, the knuckles high, hand soft, thumb bent as often referred to in Lesson II. Next, without the bow, make a series of full bow strokes in the air, down and up continuously, just above the string and in relation to each string in turn, checking all points mentioned in Lesson II.

At the furthest extreme of the down-bow, extend your reach to its maximum by actually moving (but not forcing) your shoulder-blade forward. The shoulder moves *forward* as a consequence, but should never be raised. Even though you are still not holding the bow, you should remember the backward folding and spreading of the fingers and thumb in the down-bow (fingers and thumb bending), and the gathering together of the fingers and thumb in the up-bow, without ever losing the sense of the balanced hold. Feel these movements in conjunction with the wrist and the rotation of the arm and the elbow, up and anti-clockwise in the down-bow – the opposite in the up-bow – and with the relaxed spread of the back and the action of the shoulder-blade.

EXERCISE 2

Take the bow in a light flexible hold and do the above exercise, not actually on the string, but with the bow approximately an inch above it and moving parallel to the bridge. All the details described in Lesson II should be remembered (see Diagrams 24–29, pp. 47–48), especially the raising of the wrist with fingers lengthening in the course of the up-bow (without losing their light hold of the bow) and the lowering of the wrist with fingers bending in the course of the down-bow. Although it may be a bit early to introduce preparatory movements, I would like to sow the seed with the following thought. When approaching the nut on an up-bow, by bending the thumb in the direction of the bow tip, you will facilitate the fourth finger pressure required to balance the bow, and you will also help prepare the down-bow by allowing the free momentum of the hand to be carried forward beyond the point where the wrist stops and a slight movement in the knuckles anticipates the new down-bow stroke.

EXERCISE 3

You should now be ready to sound the harmonic, together and alternating with an adjacent open string. The main aim will be to make the sound light and without shades of expression. The advantage of using two strings – one a harmonic, the other an open string – is that it combines lightness of stroke, accuracy of level and a deliberate undulation *from the very beginning*, which dissolves that unnecessary fear of touching another string! I believe in finding control not through fear and avoidance but through sensitivity, flexibility and continuous search. A further advantage of beginning with a harmonic and an open string is that before vibrato is introduced the ear can listen to a pure sound, the pitch of which can be easily rectified. Try these exercises on other pairs of strings and other harmonics, slurring the notes in groups of three or six:

There are certain problems connected with this whole-bow stroke which can be most easily demonstrated as follows.

Begin at the tip with the bow resting lightly on the A string, and all the fingers resting lightly on the bow, third and fourth fingers just barely touching. Now make a slow and even up-bow stroke the whole length of the bow, right to the nut. As the distance from the bow's tip to its contact point with the string increases, so naturally its weight bearing down on the string will increase, and an unwanted crescendo will automatically result unless a continually changing compensation is made in the bow hand. This compensation is largely the responsibility of the fourth finger (and also of the third) and, of course, of the arm from which the wrist depends. You will remember a similar situation in Lesson II, p. 33, when the stick was gradually pulled through the fingers from the middle balancing position to the normal hold at the nut.

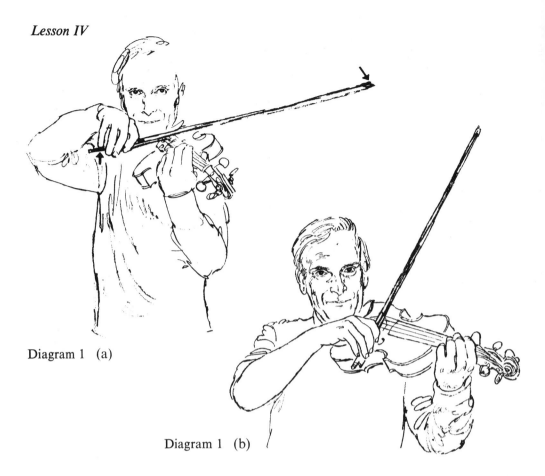

Diagram 1   (a)

Diagram 1   (b)

When the bow is in its most horizontal plane, i.e. on the G string (Diagram 1a), the increase of its weight on the string will be noticeably greater than in its most vertical plane, i.e. on the E string (Diagram 1b). The thumb and all the fingers of the right hand, except the fourth, must remain soft as they lengthen slightly throughout the up-bow stroke; the fourth finger alone increases or decreases its counter-pressure just enough to compensate for the gradual change from carrying most of the weight of the bow (lower half) to letting most of it rest on the string (upper half). Keep the elbow almost on one level except when changing strings.

Try to feel the vibrations of the string transmitted through the bow to your fingers, not only to test the sensitivity of your hold, but also to improve your awareness of minute sensations.

To develop the sensitivity of the bow fingers, hold the violin at a raised angle and feel how at a certain point the third finger prevents the bow from sliding towards the bridge. This requirement is particularly noticeable in the course of an up-bow during which the bow weight increases. As a general rule it is good to play with the violin at a slightly elevated angle. This frees the chest, neck and head and gives the performer a greater freedom and command – both over his own performance and over his audience.

The third and fourth fingers often leave the stick as it approaches the point on a down-bow, unless of course the bow has to be raised off the string. This generally happens too when playing in the upper third of the bow. The third and fourth fingers resume their balancing activity, of course, in the up-bow when approaching the lower half of the bow.

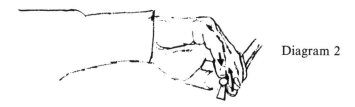

Diagram 2

EXERCISE 4

Already in Lessons II and III we have worked on the two extreme positions of a movement, beginning *in* and returning *to* a middle position. We will now practise the bow stroke in this way, dividing it into two halves instead of moving continuously through the whole stroke as in Exercises 1, 2 and 3 of this lesson. In this way, you will be most aware of the fact that it is the forearm which actively leads the stroke in the upper half of the bow, whereas the upper arm leads in the lower half as well as supporting the weight of the bow. These are smooth strokes *without momentum*, i.e. with minimal emphasis on sections A and C of my Basic Stroke. There is also no attempt to *draw* sound and therefore even section B does not actually apply in this sense. The 'hold' is soft throughout.

Now with all fingers on the bow:

(a) Do a series of half-bows between the middle and tip, starting in the middle. (The left hand should be soft and well shaped with one finger on a harmonic.) The middle is the ideal part of the bow in which to check the bow hold described in Lesson II, p. 37. Here, in the middle of the bow, the back of the hand, the wrist, and the forearm should all be approximately in a straight line and flattish, i.e. wrist neither high nor low. The wrist then lowers in the down-bow (Diagram 3) and in the up-bow rises (Diagram 4).

Diagram 3

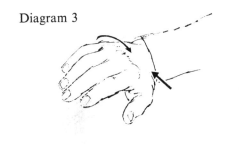

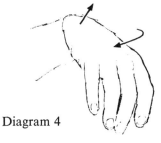

Diagram 4

The forearm in its movement away from you brings the upper arm and shoulder forward with the help of a horizontally expanding and widening back; the whole arm, as it straightens, rotates towards the first finger, and the wrist gradually gives way until it takes over from the forearm and pulls the hand towards the end of the stroke, reaching its lowest level at the tip. The fingers and thumb, already curved in the middle, gradually reach their most bent position just before the change of bow. See Diagrams 24–29, pp. 47–48.

In the opposite direction, the wrist is released upwards and the shoulder widens and relaxes backwards a little; the hand senses the pull of gravity, the fingers and thumb lengthen without losing the 'bridge' hold and the forearm pushes up, carrying the hand with it and bringing the upper arm and shoulder back to their normal position; the whole arm, as it bends, rotates back towards the fourth finger but without losing height. On reaching the middle of the bow the back of the hand, wrist and forearm should again be in an approximately straight line.

When momentum is later on introduced, the change of direction from an up-bow to a down-bow is usually marked by a reaction, sharp or soft, fast or slow in the fingers and knuckles.

(b) Next do a similar series of half-bows in the lower part of the bow, in which you must be aware of carrying a good deal of the bow's weight. This carrying is a function of both arm and fingers. There must, nevertheless, be a feeling of the hand hanging from the wrist, especially during the up-bow where the wrist reaches its highest position just before the change of bow at the heel. The elbow naturally drops slightly as the wrist rises and as the arm is folded in the up-bow. But once this adjustment is made the elbow maintains its height – sometimes even increasing it – so that it is easily able to return to its pulling function in the down-bow.

In the down-bow the elbow leads. When you are playing on the E string, gravity aids with a small inclination to fall, and when playing on the G string, i.e. on a more horizontal plane, gravity gives way to the continuous pulling of the arm. In proceeding towards the middle of the bow, the wrist is gradually lowered to its straighter position.

EXERCISE 5

The following exercise will be a useful preparation before you put these two halves together again in a continuous whole-bow stroke. Begin at the nut and draw the bow to the middle with the upper arm; after pausing briefly to check your position, continue the stroke to the tip, now leading with the forearm. During this pause at mid-stroke in the down-bow, become aware that your shoulder is soft and is preparing to move (fall) again. Rather than thinking in terms of an uncontrolled fall, I would prefer the image of *floating* forwards and of floating backwards. Maintaining height is essential to violin playing, as it is to flying; there can be no lightness, nor softness, nor range of volume in either left or right hands without this height.

Again, during the pause at mid-stroke in the up-bow, become aware that the balanced shoulder is preparing to move (fall) backwards in the remaining half of the up-bow. See Diagram 5 opposite.

Diagram 5

EXERCISE 6

You should now be ready to return to the continuous whole-bow stroke of Exercise 3 with a new awareness of that point of the bow where the upper arm becomes passive, its active role taken over by the forearm, or vice versa, the various actions flowing freely and smoothly into each other.

Although this point is approximately in the middle of the bow, it is recognised by a different feeling in the arm (each player's being determined by the length of his arm) rather than by looking for an imaginary pre-determined spot on the bow stick.

(a) Make a series of whole-bow strokes as above.

(b) Make a series of whole and half-bows in the following rhythm: ♩ ♫ ♩ ♩ ♫ The bow speed should be constant in the crotchets and quavers. Do this on our two-string harmonic and open-string intervals – on either or both strings, alternating or together.

(c) Now do the same rhythm, but with a whole-bow stroke to each note. As the bow speed will be twice as fast on the quavers as on the crotchets, you must carry more of the bow's weight on the quavers to make an even sound throughout. Develop the habit of listening critically to the sound you produce, as your ear is the ultimate guide to all the complex movements which go into making the sound you want, whether the goal is the even sound of this exercise or a more expressive one in a piece of music.

Applying weight to the stroke

Lay aside the violin and bow for a moment and try the following exercise. Place one fist against the other in front of the chest, the forearms in a diagonal line across the body so that the right arm is approximately in its playing position. Then expand the back and shoulders sideways and feel how the fists press against each other. Release this pressure by relaxing the shoulders, the right shoulder upwards, as it were, taking up the weight of the arm so that it is in its 'carried' state. The exercise can be varied by placing the backs of the hands against each other, instead of the fists, fingers pointing towards the chest. At the same time as the back is expanded the backs of

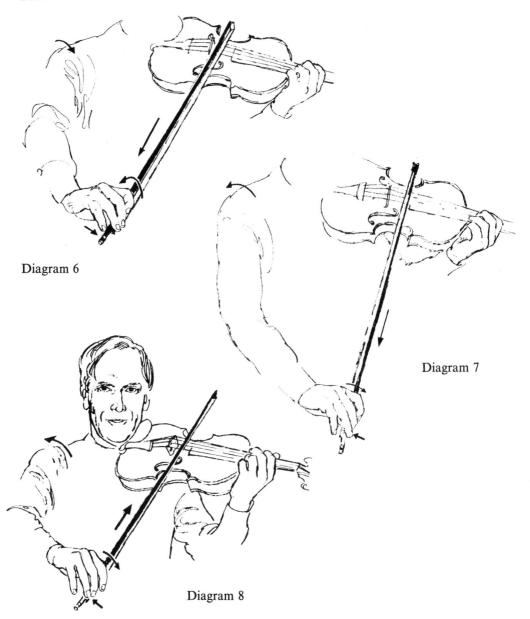

Diagram 6

Diagram 7

Diagram 8

the hands are opened outwards so that the fingers of each hand are continually in contact and are finally pressing tip against tip to form a circle with the arms, shoulders and chest. (This 'expanding circle' exercise for the right hand corresponds, in fact, to that described in Lesson III, p. 63, for left-hand pressure.)

Returning to the instrument, place one left-hand finger on a harmonic and rest the bow lightly on the string, the arm in its 'carried' state. Then exert pressure on the bow, via the right-hand fingers, by means of the 'expanding circle' action, and

78

release the pressure by taking up the weight as described above. The bow should remain on one spot and not be drawn across the string.

When we apply pressure on the bow, what we are in fact doing is to allow some of the weight of the arm to fall on to the bow, the exact amount depending on the volume of sound required (the rest of the weight is still 'carried'). This weight is transmitted through the wrist and the fingers, whose resistance to it increases the downward pressure on the bow. Most of the weight is concentrated on the first finger, whose role is therefore particularly important.

In a down-bow crescendo, particularly near the tip, the first finger can react in two different ways: (a) it can act as a grappling iron, as it were, pressing downwards and pulling the stick towards the player with the help of an outward push of the fourth finger (Diagram 6); or (b) it can press downwards and away from the player with the help of an inward pull of the third finger (Diagram 7). In the first instance the shoulder falls backwards, in the second it falls forwards. Method (a) is usually applied when the head of the violin is pointing down during the course of playing, or for a crescendo throughout a long stroke, particularly on the lower strings preceding a change of stroke to a higher string. Method (b) is usually employed when the head of the violin is pointing up, or for playing dotted rhythms on short down- and longer up-bows. These two methods are not mutually exclusive but are normally combined to achieve a balanced pressure.

In an up-bow crescendo the first finger tends to press away from the player, again with the help of the inward pull of the third finger (Diagram 8).

The application of weight and pressure inevitably brings a sense of solidarity in the hand and an increase in the opposition of the thumb to the fingers.

Play open strings with slow, loud whole bows (up and down) and become aware of the resistance of the string, which is felt all the way through the arm into the shoulder-blade. One feels the backward, forward and downward movements of the shoulder-blade particularly strongly in this type of bowing, because the arm is moving slowly in one piece (Diagrams 9 and 10).

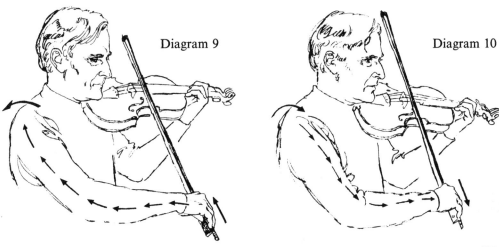

Diagram 9

Diagram 10

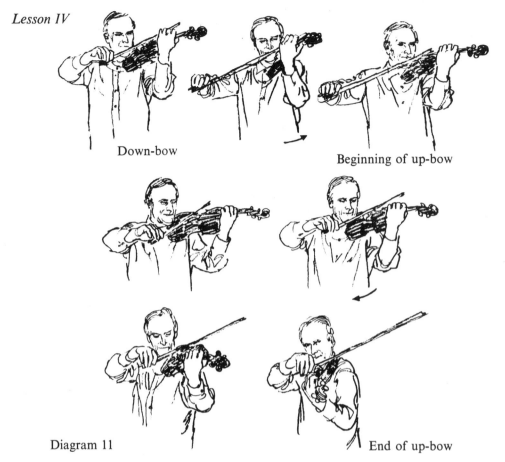

Down-bow

Beginning of up-bow

Diagram 11

End of up-bow

Sympathetic movement of the body

The horizontal swing of the body occurs in sympathy with the right-hand rather than the left-hand action, and always starts just before a change of bow. The instrument swings in the *same* direction as the bow stroke but changes direction *after* the body-swing begins and *before* the bow change. At the end of a long stroke, the body-swing has two functions:

(a) To help the completion of the stroke;

(b) To anticipate the new stroke in the opposite direction.

It is possible to view the long stroke as composed of three parts, a useful but extreme simplification: in the first part of the down-bow the body (and violin) and the stroke move in the same direction, clockwise; in the second part the stroke continues but the body returns to a middle position; in the third part the stroke continues, the body turning anti-clockwise in anticipation of the change of direction – first of the violin, then of the bow – into an up-bow.

The same analysis can be applied to the up-bow, which begins with the body already turning anti-clockwise in the direction of the up-bow; the body then returns to its middle position while the stroke continues; and finally, before the change of stroke it rotates clockwise to meet the oncoming hand in the up-bow, anticipating

80

the imminent change of direction – first of the violin, then of the bow – into the down-bow. The timing of this latter body-swing in the opposite direction to the stroke occurs, of course, sooner in fast short strokes than it does in the slower long stroke.

This swing originates in the ball of that foot which is resisting the impetus of the stroke. Thus, the down-bow is hurled, as it were, against the right foot where it meets growing resistance. In a vigorous stroke using the whole bow one should feel that the up-bow begins in the right foot; it is at that point where the foot pushes the floor away that the opposite swing begins, which, as we have seen, takes place at the end of the down-bow in anticipation of the up-bow.

The reverse occurs at the end of a vigorous up-bow when the impetus of the body is thrown against the left foot. This sensation is more marked when playing on the G string, requiring a horizontal stroke. When playing on the E string with dash and momentum, body co-ordination requires a vertical element as well – a slight rising on toes connected with the up-bow.

There is a sympathetic adjustment which occurs in the instrument. The head of the violin, which can be seen moving with the body in the direction of the stroke at the beginning of each stroke, should be raised vertically as the down-bow approaches the point and somewhat lowered as the up-bow approaches the nut. As we have seen there is also a horizontal adjustment. The student must be warned against exaggeration in actual performance.

Role of arm, hand and fingers in string-crossing

We now come to the role of the arm, hand and fingers in string-crossing. Here a vertical adjustment is combined with the horizontal movement of down- and up-bow strokes to produce a wave action similar to that of a horizontal ribbon moving up and down after being shaken.

We considered earlier the role of the thumb in horizontal movement; we will now consider the thumb in its other capacity as the principal element, the fulcrum, in string-crossing and in accents, in which function it often criss-crosses the stroke reflexes described above. If the bow is moved from a higher string to a lower without any stroke and only by the aid of the fingers and wrist, it will be noticed that the thumb is always in a bent (folded) shape on the higher string and straightens out on the lower. This can also occur on a stroke naturally enough if the down-bow is on the higher string. However, in actual playing, this depends not only (a) on the stroke, but (b) on the elbow level.

I have already mentioned the importance of preserving the 'middle position', that is, a position which allows a margin of movement and adjustment on either side. For instance, if we draw the bow on the A and D strings with a soft, middle position hold of the bow we will be able to move either to the higher E string or to the lower G string using that very margin I described, and return to our middle hold on the A and D strings.

When the string-crossings are left entirely to the fingers and the wrists, the thumb is indeed always bent on the upper string and straightened on the lower. This move-

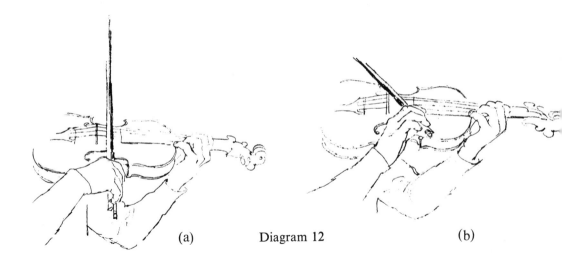

(a) Diagram 12 (b)

ment, however, does not allow the same part of the bow-hair to remain in constant contact with whichever string is being played. The sound is therefore not homogeneous, the left side of the bow-hair touching the lower string (Diagram 12a) and in the opposite way the right side of the bow-hair touching the upper string (b). To achieve a smooth sound the forearm and indeed the whole arm must join the wave action, adjusting to the string levels.

As a general rule the wider the string-crossing (as from E to G over the four strings) the more the wrist proportion of the action increases in relation to that of the arm. However, when we wish to accent or stress a note, we must return to the basic down-bow position appropriate to the particular plane of the string, be it higher or lower. This is where the arm is involved. Using the whole arm, try undulating over two strings in the course of the stroke, stressing first the finger movement, then adding the wrist and finally the forearm.

It can be observed when playing very soft détaché strokes, soft not only in sound but also in the feelings of the joints, that the thumb is indeed joining the first finger against the other three in the down-bow and, conversely, joining the third and fourth fingers against the first and second in the up-bow. But as soon as pressure or weight is applied in the up-bow, the thumb naturally counteracts this pressure. Now, the thumb, when assuming an active rather than a passive role, resumes its *basic* position, bent towards the tip of the bow.

Both forms of pressure at the point – the basic one of the bow stick pulled towards the body, and the other one with the bow stick pushed away – should be practised in string-crossings to cultivate the spring gathered from the note preceding the crossing. The upper arm should fall on the supporting 'bridge' in the hand when the crossing is from a lower string to an upper string, or should get its spring from the fingers in order to be thrown from an upper to a lower string. As I have already said, a bent thumb in the up-bow before the crossing allows elbow and shoulder to relax and fall, as it were, from the wrist after the initial finger lengthening in the up-bow stroke. This applies particularly to crossings from an up-bow on a lower string to a down-bow on an upper string. In the opposite crossing the arm leads, continuing, as it were, its up-bow direction to bring it to the new string level. This movement produces a smooth crossing from upper to lower string – provided the fourth finger is trained to catch the weight at the moment of crossing. If the lower string or strings are only to be sounded momentarily, for instance when a legato melody on the E string is accompanied by occasional chords on the lower three strings, the arm should remain on the E string level and the bow allowed to drop on to the lower strings by a momentary release of the counter-balancing pressure in the fourth finger.

Return frequently to the main basic hold so as to avoid exaggerated finger, knuckle or wrist movement. It is generally preferable in string changes to use more arm movement and less finger movement in order to maintain the evenness of sound and the same bow hair in contact with the string. Take care also that the thumb action does not affect the dominant position of the knuckles, i.e. lowering in the course of the down-bow and lifting in the course of the up-bow.

Bowing strokes

Let us now begin building our genealogy of bowing strokes. Although it is possible to do the following exercises on open strings, I would much prefer to hold a note with any of the four left-hand fingers on one of the strings and as soon as the student is able to he should hold a second note on an adjoining string, to form thirds, seconds, fourths, octaves; these should be used later in scale form. Check left-hand flexibility from time to time. Unused fingers must be kept *soft*. Later, when actually playing, it is essential to feel and maintain extreme softness in the finger *about* to play.

Slurred string-crossing

EXERCISE 1

Our first exercise will be a waving stroke over two strings, five notes to each stroke. The arrows above the notes refer to the knuckle elevations and the curved arrows below the notes refer to the thumb positions. In the down-bow the knuckles tend towards the depressed position and in the up-bow towards the protruded position. Here again, remember that this generalised statement does not mean that the knuckles remain in one depressed or in one protruding position, but that in the course of the down-bow they move towards a depressed position and that even this general direction has its own little ups and downs as the bow crosses between two strings. It is for this very reason, in fact, that I want to begin with the waving movement. The lower arrows indicate how the thumb alternates between its bent position, rolling towards the tip of the bow, on the upper string, and the opposite roll as the bow moves to the lower string. This is a passive, and not an active adjustment.

Lesson IV

Play this exercise with the whole length of the bow on each group of five notes; play it as well on the three pairs of strings A and D, D and G, and finally E and A. It should be even with no accents on any one note.

You will notice that in the up-bow the thumb rolls slightly away from the tip, but moves vertically at least as much as horizontally. This is co-ordinated with a slightly rising wrist (or falling hand) and slightly lengthening fingers. Never lose the sensation of the 'bridge' in the right hand and develop a real sense of contact between the fingers and the stick which should gradually develop into a firm and flexible hold. We stated that the thumb rolls the bow at the beginning of the up-bow stroke in an anti-clockwise direction (remember that this is as seen from the bottom end of the bow looking towards the tip). This is more of a sensation, a feeling, than an 'observable' effect, because the anti-clockwise thumb-roll is compensated for by the slightly rising wrist rolling the bow in the opposite direction; the net effect is virtually no *observable* roll of the bow! By the same token the second finger is helping the thumb by pressing the bow against the thumb in a clockwise direction to secure a greater contact; because of these opposing pressures there is little visible evidence of action.

Remember it is advisable to use not open strings but a fingered interval. I prefer thirds (or fourths) as these oblige the left hand to maintain a healthy, elevated position over and around the fingerboard. Every so often the left hand and arm should be checked for passive softness. The left hand should be kept lifted from the elbow – left shoulder relaxed, falling down and backwards.

Slurred string-crossing with accent

EXERCISE 2

This can only follow after Exercise 1 has been mastered. Here I have added stresses or accents to the first and third notes of each group of five notes. The fifth note is not accented to allow preparation for the accent on the first note of the following group. The fifth note should, in fact, be soft and flow smoothly into the new stroke.

We have said that as a general rule the right shoulder 'floats' forwards on the down-bow to make space for the strokes, and backwards on the up-bow for the same reason. However, when we wish to apply weight for the purpose of stress or volume we must slightly restrain this floating forwards or backwards to 'pull' the weight of the shoulder in the down-bow and to 'push' the weight of the shoulder in the up-bow. These feelings should be co-ordinated with the differing degrees of the 'carrying' of the arm required for soft and loud strokes.

In this exercise we are accenting the notes in which the thumb finds itself more especially in the 'normal' position of the particular stroke: somewhat bent and

84

rolling towards the tip in the down-bow, and somewhat elongated and rolling in the opposite direction in the up-bow. You will notice that the knuckles tend to depress a little more on the accented notes in the down-bow, and rise in relation to the finger-tips a little more on the accented notes in the up-bow than on the unaccented ones.

If we were to give accents to the second and fourth notes on the lower string, there would be a little more finger-work on the accents because the basic arm level is associated with the three-note majority on the higher string. If the last note of the second group were also accented, there would be more arm movement, because the arm level is associated with the majority of notes on the lower strings.

EXERCISE 3
In this exercise we reverse the stroke; we begin on the lower string, and we play the exercise without accents as we did in Exercise 1. The importance of this exercise lies in the opposite rotation of the string changes. Thus in changing from down-bow to up-bow at the tip, the arm falls instead of having to rise, as in Exercise 1, and at the nut, it has to rise before the down-bow instead of falling as it did in Exercise 1.

You will notice that this latter rotation at the nut will require a very fine sensitivity to weight in the arm and a very delicate sensitivity to the balance of the bow in the fingers. Do study the minute adjustments which must be made in the fingers and the wrist to maintain a straight bow, parallel to the bridge, and above all a smooth sound in this change of stroke at the nut. In moving from the A string to the D string at the nut (from the up-bow to the down-bow, that is) the bow must not be allowed to fall on the lower string because of the weight of its length – the fourth finger has to carry that weight and ensure that the bow remains parallel to the bridge. In fact, at the beginning of the down-bow you should be playing with the bow on the outer hair rather than on the inner (Diagram 13). When the bow is drawn further up into the hand at the change of direction this becomes less necessary.

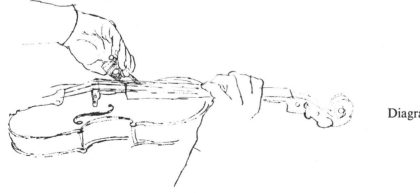

Diagram 13

Lesson IV

EXERCISE 4

Now we will apply the stressed or accented note in the same way as we did in Exercise 2. In the groups of five notes we again accent only the first and third, leaving the fifth unaccented to prepare more easily for the accent on the first note of the following group.

When beginning on the lower string with accents on the lower notes, you will find you will want to bend the thumb as for the accents on the higher notes. To do this the elbow will have to rise comparatively higher to enable the hand to adopt the same position.

Dotted rhythms in detached bowing

EXERCISE 5

In this exercise we introduce a dotted rhythm into the stroke.

Beginning with the five notes as we use them in Exercise 1 in the down-bow, on the two alternate notes on the lower string we take very quick, smooth, short and light up-bows which hardly interrupt the whole bow stroke. Conversely, in the up-bow the two notes on the upper string are taken in very fast light down-bows which again hardly interrupt the stroke. Now we are really beginning to develop the wavelike movement to the point where it will unlock all the others!

EXERCISE 6

The same dotted rhythm as in Exercise 5, but beginning on the lower string in the pattern of Exercise 3. Use whole down-bow on the first five notes; whole up-bow on the second five notes. Divide the bow evenly, using little on the short notes.

EXERCISES 7 AND 8

Exercises 5 and 6 can now be varied. In these variations we use a long and fast stroke on the short note, and a very short and slow stroke on the long note. This enables us to use the whole length of the bow on each group of five notes as we did in the previous exercises. It also teaches us to play with various speeds of the bow.

86

Preparation for the Retake

Exercise 9

Now for the first time we will begin interrupting the sound, i.e. interrupting the continuous contact of the bow with the string.

As in Exercise 1, draw your bow over the five notes of the down-bow in a continuous smooth stroke. Now do the same without playing the notes on the lower string. In other words, leave the upper string as if you were going to play the lower string, but do not allow the bow actually to touch the lower string. The opposite applies to the up-bow during which you will sound the three notes on the lower string, omitting the two notes on the upper string. You will be using the same movements of the arm, wrist and fingers, but assuming for instance you are playing on the A and D strings, you will not be going as far as the D string during the down-bow or as far as the A string during the up-bow. The lift must occur in the same wave-like pattern as if you were going to *play* the silent notes. What you will hear will be:

The notes heard should be played smoothly and quietly, without accents.

Exercise 10

This is the same as Exercise 9 but beginning the down-bow on the lower string and the up-bow on the higher string. Remember to check thumb and knuckle movements. In this exercise you will hear only the three lower notes in the down-bow and the three upper notes in the up-bow.

Lesson IV

Détaché

EXERCISE 11

Here we take one stroke to each note, all strokes being even in length and using the same section of the bow. We will do these next exercises on three pairs of strings as in the previous exercises, and in the four quarters of the bow. We will begin as we did in Exercise 1 with the down-bow on the upper string, as follows:

In détaché strokes alternating between two strings observe not only the different vertical movements occurring in the down-bow beginning on the upper string and in the down-bow beginning on the lower string, but also that the longer horizontal stroke is associated naturally with the former and the greater vertical movement with the latter. The bow has to be controlled at the nut where it is heaviest over and during a wider fall. In this stroke we must have very fine control of the bow to avoid a scratch on the lower strings.

One of the most useful exercises is to practice the détaché at the nut. There are two extreme forms with infinite degrees of speed, strength and length of stroke in between. The first form is at moderate speed, involving arm motion almost exclusively, no wrist/finger motion, no momentum. We use about a quarter of the bow, keeping the bow in a balanced hold without strain, the hand hanging, but not loosely. The other form consists of very fast, small short bows using soft wrist and soft fingers with proportionately less arm motion. Here the arm motion is reduced to an undulating wave action.

EXERCISE 12

The same beginning with the down-bow on the lower string of the pair.

You will notice that the amplitude of the wrist movement is greater in Exercise 11 than in Exercise 12. Assuming again that you are playing on the A and D strings, this is because the lower plane of the arm on the A string is added to the lower wrist plane of the down-bow. And in Exercise 12 the amplitude of the wrist movement is correspondingly diminished because the higher plane of the arm on the D string is in this case *subtracted* from the lower plane of the wrist (and knuckles) in the down-bow. Practise Exercises 11 and 12 *pp*, *p* and *mf*.

EXERCISE 13

This is the same as Exercise 11, only this time the down-bows in the first group of five notes are loud and the up-bows soft, and in the second group the up-bows are loud and the down-bows soft. The last note of each group should be soft, the better to prepare the *forte* on the new stroke.

EXERCISE 14

This resembles Exercise 13, but begins with the down-bow on the lower string.

Remember to do Exercises 13 and 14 on three pairs of strings, and in the four quarters of the bow. Play them also in the following rhythms:

The Retake

EXERCISE 15

This is patterned on Exercise 13, but you will sound only the *forte* notes and not touch the string for the *piano* notes. It should make the same sound as you heard in Exercise 9. These are the first retakes proper. You will notice that it becomes increasingly difficult to play these notes towards the tip of the bow. Here great finger control and complete relaxation from the shoulder is required to place the bow quietly on the string and to draw a certain length of stroke. When working on these retakes in the upper part of the bow, you may also use very short falling or bounced strokes. Feel that the bow actually falls and is caught again in the fingers.

In fast up-bows, the thumb plus second and first fingers are usually sufficient, except when *first* lifting the bow off the string before the throw or bounce takes over when the other fingers are important as well.

Remember that when the bow falls on the string, it bounces off due to the combined elasticity of string, stick and hair, and that the fewer the fingers that remain on the stick, the freer the bow is to bounce. But the second and first fingers, which hold the bow and may be nearly touching, must have a good and flexible hold, as they actually push the bow in an up-bow on each retake.

The place on the bow where the retakes are done is very critical, depending on speed and length of sound and volume desired. Basically, the nearer the nut, the slower, longer and louder the strokes, and the more third-finger balancing is required. Conversely, the nearer the tip, the more bouncy, short and dry, and the softer is the sound.

The best average spot (as for the last movement of the Mendelssohn Concerto) is (a) low enough on the bow for the elbow to point downwards while the wrist may fall with the fingers and hand producing actual retake (further up on the bow the wrist angle is such that no pleasant-sounding stroke can be produced); yet (b) high enough to enjoy some natural bounce and good speed and lightness, high enough also to enable only second and first fingers and thumb to be used. The wrist must always be soft.

EXERCISE 16

The same as Exercise 14, but beginning with the down-bows on the lower string as in Exercise 13; only the *fortes* are audible and the sound and rhythm you hear should be similar to Exercise 10.

EXERCISE 17

This is like Exercise 13, but the stroke is long and the return inaudible stroke is very fast. The fast stroke is an upbeat, as it were, to the sounded long stroke.

EXERCISE 18

This resembles Exercise 17 but begins with the down-bow on the lower string.

Interrupted bowings (Martelé)

EXERCISE 19

With this exercise we begin the interrupted bows. Our new series continues on two strings, and we slur two notes at a time, stopping the bow between each pair. This is the beginning of the sharp accent, the cutting attack, of martelé and staccato. Before proceeding to the exercise, I want to explain the principle of the sharp accent. The sudden attack comes from a release of built-up pressure at the very beginning of the stroke. The pressure is built up as follows. We go into the stroke softly without sounding the note, all the joints of the right arm from the shoulder to the fingers soft. Pressure is then applied by allowing the arm weight to be concentrated on the first finger, which will tend to move slightly up the stick, with the corresponding increase in the counter-pressure of the thumb. We are now holding the bow very firmly and its pressure on the string prevents its moving. At this moment we release the pressure; we dissolve the resistance in the fingers (sometimes even lifting the fourth and third fingers) and allow the arm to pull the bow with a very fast initial tug. It cannot be emphasised sufficiently that the martelé is in fact a release of pressure previously applied.

For this, a firm grip on the bow must be developed, but be careful that this firmness is not allowed to interfere with the softness of the wrist, which should always be maintained.

To come now specifically to our first exercise, we begin each slurred pair of notes softly, ending abruptly on the louder, lower note. In the up-bow we begin with a lower string, again softly, stopping the stroke abruptly on the upper string, each time making a crescendo from *piano* to *forte*.

This method obliges us to begin each short stroke softly. The pauses should be as long as necessary to ensure the complete dispersal of tension and its replacement by balance.

This, and the following exercises, are done on whole bows.

EXERCISE 20

This is the same as Exercise 19, but begins with a down-bow on the lower string of a pair.

Lesson IV

EXERCISE 21

To train attack, this time we begin the first note sforzato with a diminuendo to the second stopped note of each pair. Remember to release the pressure on the bow and on the string at the beginning of each stroke and to return to the relaxed state. The pause between the pairs should be long enough to build up the firmness in tension, preceding the release.

We should, however, note in passing that to achieve an even stronger and sharper attack in the martelé stroke, we can begin in the air and land on the string when the bow is already moving. The movement here is that described for whole bows with free-swinging arm, Lesson II, p. 44.

EXERCISE 22

This is the same as Exercise 20, but begins with a down-bow on the lower string with the up-bow on the upper string.

Exercises 19, 20, 21 and 22 may also be done with three, four or five-and-a-half pairs of waves to the stroke, not only as we have been describing, which is two-and-a-half pairs or five notes to the whole bow.

Further Retakes

Now we will return to retakes, but this time with very short strokes instead of longish strokes. In the following exercises I would like you to imagine the very short stroke as belonging to a somewhat more complex pattern of strokes which is not sounded.

Imagine you were playing the first three notes of Exercise 11, p. 88, but were in fact sounding only the first note. You would be actually making a complete wave of the wrist and fingers in the air, following the sounded note, and you would end up in the same position in which you started, i.e. a down-bow position, in a state of repose. The preparation for another sounded down-bow note would be a very fast up-bow, unsounded in the air.

EXERCISES 23 AND 24

Beginning on the lower string, these should be done in this rhythmic pattern, in the same way as the longer retakes were done in Exercises 15 and 16.

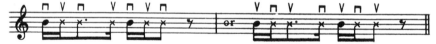

The up-bow version of 23 follows the same rhythmic wave pattern as I have described for the down-bow except for its being in the opposite direction; in other words, the moment of repose following the short note and the one complete wave movement occurs after the up-bow in the air, and the next short up-bow sound is preceded by a very fast down-bow in the air. These exercises are for training the very fast reflex actions which are required in handling the bow.

In Exercise 24 we will apply the same principle as the ones we had in Exercise 23 but on a different rhythmic wave pattern. Our point of repose will be on the up-bow in the air immediately preceding the short sounded down-bow. The rhythmic pattern differs, but the succession of movements is the same. There is one complete down-bow wave consisting of three parts, as if you were playing very quickly the first three notes of Exercise 11 followed immediately by the relaxed resting up-bow in the air.

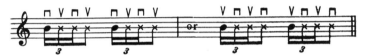

Repeat Exercises 23 and 24 but with a martelé attack, the sudden starting of the bow from the string itself. Remember it is a relaxation of pressure. Eventually you will be able to do retakes giving each note this sharp incisive attack. The sounded note should not be loud for our purpose. The softer it is, the more control and the better release of pressure you prove.

Speed in string-crossing

EXERCISES 25 AND 26
These exercises should be practised on our basic series of string pairs.

They are the same as Exercises 17 and 18, but in a fast dotted rhythm with fast and slow strokes alternating. The bow does not leave the strings and thus produces a continuous sound. Practise them in the three thirds of the bow, in the two halves, and even with whole bows.

EXERCISES 27 AND 28

In these exercises the notes are short and the bow is in the air between each pair of fast sounds. We do this in three thirds of the bow.

Different intervals for the bowing exercises

EXERCISE 29

It will be a great relief to the violinist at this stage if he can use a variety of intervals. He is already using three pairs of strings. If he is playing in thirds, he can use fingers 1 and 3, or 2 and 4. If he is playing in fourths, he can use fingers 1 and 2, or 2 and 3, or 3 and 4. But he should also play in octaves using fingers 1 and 4, and best of all, if his hand is flexible enough, he should use the interval of the unison with finger 1 on the upper string and finger 4 on the lower string. These latter, octave and unison, are a wonderful training for the automatic adjustment of the fingers to the demands of intonation.

Different Martelé strokes

EXERCISES 30 AND 31

These will be martelé strokes both on the down-bow and the up-bow, the bow remaining on the string, but completely passive and quiet between strokes. Remember that the martelé is a release and at the same time an attack.

These two exercises should be done in the two halves of the bow and with whole-bow strokes. When the student can play scales he should apply this stroke to his scales.

EXERCISE 32
In Exercise 32 we will combine the whole-bow martelé (which we have done in Exercises 30 and 31) with the fast upbeat which we have done in Exercises 25 and 26.

Immediately before each martelé stroke, after the bow has stopped at the end of the previous martelé, there will be a very short, fast note. This will make a dotted rhythm using the whole bow. It should also be practised in halves, thirds and quarters of the bow.

EXERCISE 33
This is the same, beginning on the lower string.

EXERCISE 34
This is the opposite of Exercises 32 and 33, in that the bow is carried along its whole length without touching the string and plays two very short and fast notes alternating at each end; down/up at the tip; up/down at the nut – and more difficult,. down/up at the nut followed by up/down at the extreme point. This requires a mobile shoulder action.

Of course, this is a very useful exercise for spiccato, to which we will soon be coming.

Ricochet
EXERCISE 35
We are now ready to take the ricochet exercises started in Lesson II (p. 43) several stages further.
We begin by learning how to control the number, speed and height of the bounces. Deliberately drawing the bow somewhat slower than in our first efforts, we 'catch' the stroke after, say, four bounces, by lifting it off the string with fourth finger pressure

combined with a sharp stroke in the opposite direction. If we repeat this we get a pattern as follows:

We first vary this by starting up-bow. Then we vary the speed of the horizontal stroke. We try different speeds of stroke at different parts of the bow, discovering which speed goes best at each part. We try varying degrees of pressure on the fourth finger, which result in the bow being released from varying heights. We try six, eight, twelve or even sixteen bounces and experiment with varying the speed of the horizontal stroke while the bow is actually bouncing, thus obtaining a rallentando or accelerando within one ricochet series.

Transition to Spiccato

EXERCISE 36

In the next stage we arrive at continuous bouncing:

We try varying strengths of impulse on the first of each four, aiming at reducing it to an absolute minimum. It should be possible with practice to get sufficient impulse to keep the bounce going from the almost imperceptible change of inclination in the

hand between up- and down-bow. We then play in threes

and in twos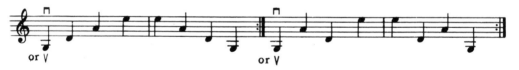

ending up with a plain up- and down-bow spiccato which we try out at varying speeds and at different parts of the bow. We should make no conscious attempt at altering the state of wrist and fingers which has been arrived at during the course of these exercises.

Spiccato

EXERCISE 37

It is as well to practise this basic spiccato on string-crossings as follows, bearing in mind that the change in level is made with the whole arm.

Repeat each note four times, then twice, then three times, then singly as written, starting first down- then up-bow.

EXERCISE 38

Before trying to modify the rather hard nature of this basic spiccato, we will now revert to the ricochet, this time combined with crossing over two strings, because the mechanism involved is an enlarged, more easily sensed version of that involved in the softer spiccato types.

In the following exercise, instead of catching the ricochet with a sharp stroke in the opposite direction combined with a pressure lift from the fourth finger, we intend to put the bow down on the neighbouring string smoothly, draw a note of a fair length and then start the next ricochet group with a smooth take-off from the string, instead of releasing it from above the string.

Start without any ricochet at all:

The arm is on a level appropriate to playing on both strings at once, and the change of level is done with wrist and fingers only.

We then exaggerate the size of the crossing movement and give a small jerk or flick before the bounced notes, releasing the fingers immediately. At the end of the ricochet we replace the bow on the neighbouring string by slightly increasing the hold of the fingers so that the bouncing tendency is damped. By beginning in this way with six or eight bounces, one has more time to feel the subtle adjustments in

muscle-tone necessary to produce this effect. Once this feel has been acquired, it is a simple matter to reduce the number of bounces, acquiring on the way control over

the common violinistic figuration:

The same correlation between speed of bounce and speed of horizontal stroke holds good for this type of ricochet. A hint of the string-crossing movement remains when this type of stroke is performed on one string. The movement is still a wave but a shallower one.

It will be noticed that the up-bow ricochet of this type needs a greater impulse to get it going and indeed, with six or eight bounces, a certain amount of help is needed to *keep* it going. We suggest giving this help through a version of the up-bow position of the hand (Diagram 22, p. 42) exaggerated to the point of tilting the stick well away from the player. With the hand in this position, it will be found that the bounces 'echo' in a tendency of the forearm to roll with the bounces. This tendency should be reinforced by adding a voluntary roll to the passive one, a fairly subtle feat of co-ordination. In this way, it will be found possible to continue the up-bow bounces to a point surprisingly near the heel. We have here crossed the border between ricochet and flying staccato.

Our softened ricochet points the way towards a softened spiccato. It might be objected that this is a roundabout way of approaching a simple stroke, but in fact what appears to be the more complicated stroke, the ricochet, is easier to produce because, having set off the bounce by means of one or other of the methods discussed, there is nothing more to do except draw the bow at the desired speed. With those spiccato types, however, which are produced in a part of the bow in which it is necessary to support partially its weight, this carrying element can frequently lead to trouble because (a) the bow is carried with such a firm grip that the natural bounce is eliminated, and the bow has to be deliberately thrown; (b) the firm grip interferes with the compensatory movement of wrist and fingers which keeps the bow parallel with the bridge, so that the bow strikes the string at different angles on up- and down-bows, thus aggravating the unevenness caused by the deliberate throw.

Transition from Spiccato to Détaché

Now, with our basic, rather hard spiccato, we should have arrived at a relation between arm, wrist and fingers such that, although the compensatory movement does take place and the bow remains parallel, there is practically no other re-active movement in wrist and fingers. In other words, the whole length of the stroke is covered by the arm. If we now allow the hand to carry out a gentler version of the whip-like action with which we set our smooth take-off ricochet going in both directions, we find that the stroke softens in direct proportion to the softness in wrist and fingers, until it finally comes to earth in the form of a smooth détaché in the lower half. It is an essential pre-condition of this transition exercise that we keep to the same length of arm movement while gradually releasing the tension in wrist and fingers. If we do not, i.e. if we cut down on the amount of arm movement while allowing wrist and fingers more play, we will actually increase the bounce until, at the point at which the arm is virtually stationary and wrist and fingers in a state of complete 'flop', the bounce becomes uncontrollable. The adjustment of the proportion of arm movement to hand movement gives us in fact one reliable means of adjusting the degree of bounce. In practice, the degree of bounce can also be altered by adjusting the tilt of the bow or by changing the part of the bow at which the stroke is performed. The choice of these methods depends on speed, dynamic level and expressive context.

Rapid Spiccato (Sautillé)

This adjustment takes on a different significance in the faster spiccato strokes in which the length added by the whip-like movement of the hand means that the arm movement can be correspondingly reduced. This makes the performance of extended fast spiccato passages far less tiring. One can best take advantage of this wrist and finger movement if the arm is tilted inwards sufficiently for the up and down wrist movement to be brought into the plane of the stroke without impeding the fingers' reaction to the horizontal movement. In order to encourage this whip-like action, short martelé strokes produced by only fingers and wrist are often helpful. This action is illustrated in Diagrams 15 and 16 in Lesson II, p. 39.

The sustained stroke

Perhaps the most important stroke in violin playing is the one that produces a rich, sustained sound, section B of the Basic Stroke (p. 71). In this sphere, I would like to point out that it is not the pressure on the string which is the final object but rather the amplitude, i.e. the width of the actual vibrations on the string which are set in motion by the bow. It can readily be observed that too great a pressure will crush these vibrations. This is easily tested if we draw the bow with excess pressure nearer the fingerboard. Here, where the natural vibration of the open string is widening perceptibly and by the same token losing power, the sound can be easily crushed by excessive pressure. Conversely, when the bow is drawn too close to the bridge, that is, at a point where the string vibration is very tight and narrow but very powerful, the bow stroke accelerates these vibrations instead of crushing them and slowing them down, as is the case when it is too near the fingerboard. The resultant sound is a kind of whistling effect known as ponticello, from *ponte* meaning bridge. Therefore to draw a warm and beautiful sound on the violin, it is necessary: (a) to choose that spot at which the vibrations of the string have exactly the right amplitude. This depends on the length of the vibrating string, for when we play in higher positions, the vibrating portion of the string becomes successively shorter and the proportions shorten as well; (b) to apply the right pressure sufficient to set the string in motion and maintain the vibrations without crushing them; (c) to draw the bow at a precise right angle to the string.

In short accents the added pressure is applied in the direction of the stroke, but when we have to hold on to long sustained *forte* notes in a whole bow in longish strokes, this pressure is achieved by the fingers resisting the direction of the stroke (section B of our Basic Stroke).

EXERCISE 39

Now to come to Exercise 39. Using two strings, we hold one note continuously and play the other note at rhythmic intervals. The hold of the bow must be firm enough to play two strings at once, or even three as we shall see later, and yet flexible enough to obey all the injunctions relating to bow direction, string crossing and pressures we have learned in the past exercises. The down-bow version should be practised holding the upper note continuously and playing the lower note intermittently, three, four or five to the stroke. On the up-bow version do the same, holding the lower note continuously and playing the upper note intermittently. The intermittent notes should not be too short.

Lesson IV

You will notice that this exercise derives from Exercises 1 and 3. But in fact, we are climbing up another branch of bow technique.

EXERCISE 40
This is the same as 39, but inverted in that on the down-bow we hold the lower note continuously and play the upper note intermittently, and on the up-bow we play the upper note continuously and the lower note intermittently.

Exercises 39 and 40 are to be practised with slow bows *forte*, with a firm and elastic hold, long and smooth.

EXERCISE 41
The same principle, but on three strings.

This requires a very strong grip on the bow, still flexible of course. In the down-bow version we hold the upper two notes together, playing intermittently on the lowest string, and in the up-bow version we play the two lower strings continuously and the highest string intermittently.

To sound three strings simultaneously a point of contact for the bow should be chosen at which the amount of pressure required to bring the middle string into alignment with the other two is consistent with the volume and tone-quality desired. Obviously, the nearer to the fingerboard we play, the less the pressure needed to achieve this alignment. But there is another factor – the stiffness of the stick. Try sustaining a three-note chord with a very tight bow, and you will find that much less pressure is needed. Though I do not recommend a tight bow, I believe a similar effect can be obtained by holding the stick particularly firmly. We must, nevertheless, always retain elasticity in the right-hand fingers.

EXERCISE 42
This is the opposite. Beginning with a down-bow, we hold the two lower strings continuously, playing the highest string intermittently, and in the up-bow we hold the two higher strings, playing the lower string intermittently.

PRACTICE OF SUSTAINED STROKE EXERCISES

All these exercises (39–42) are important in training the arm and the reflexes of the fingers, for they enable these reflexes to continue alternating without interruption, and it is an excellent preparation not only for string-crossing, but also for bow changes, since you take the bow off one string before making the change.

The exercises should also be practised in pairs. The first exercise should always begin down-bow on the upper string, and the second exercise should always begin down-bow on the lower string.

At this point we should also do some two-string exercises with an even number of notes (6, 4 and 2) to each stroke. The importance of these lie in their introducing a figure-8 movement into the stroke, which greatly increases flexibility.

Staccato

We now come to the staccato exercises. This is a stroke that requires both great firmness and great elasticity. It is a combination of our interrupted series of sounds (Exercise 9, etc.) and of our sustained firmly held sounds (Exercises 39 and 40).

EXERCISE 43

In a single bow, first down, then up, play a sequence of a sustained note followed by a group of three fast notes in one seizure, as it were. The sustained note should be held long enough for the arm to relax completely after these seizures, the sound remaining continuous.

Play this exercise with groups of four, five, six or more fast notes.

EXERCISE 44

This is the same as Exercise 43, but after the group of fast notes the sound is interrupted and the arm relaxes during a rest.

This exercise also should be played with groups of four or more fast notes.

101

Lesson IV

Two further varieties of Staccato

As distinct from the usually uncontrollable staccato produced by a deliberate tensing of the upper arm muscles to the point of spasm, a staccato controllable up to a respectable speed can be produced in a number of different ways of which I recommend the following two as being relatively easy to acquire.

The first type is produced by a rotation movement of the forearm of which we have already had a foretaste in the assisted up-bow ricochet with smooth take-off (p. 97) which, we suggested, really amounted to a flying staccato.

By adding a little arm weight to this stroke and making the forearm roll more vigorous, we arrive at a firm up-bow staccato, the speed of which can be altered by adjusting the amplitude of the roll. In the slower stroke, the length covered by the forearm roll is supplemented by allowing the bow to be carried a certain distance with the whole arm; then the forearm is rolled inward again in preparation for the next impulse. As we get faster, this whole arm movement is cut down until we reach a point at which the bow is moved by the forearm roll alone.

It is often helpful to approach this variety of staccato from another angle, by means of a portato stroke in which the bow is not actually stopped, but is given a wave impulse by a forearm roll which is superimposed upon a normal slowish legato stroke, covering roughly the upper two-thirds of the bow.

We suggest starting with portato crotchets, up- and down-bow at a gentle pace ($\textbf{J}$ = 60):

We then do portato quavers, covering the same amount of bow:

In the next stage, without increasing the speed of our quavers, we reduce the length of bow covered to, say, the upper half. If the forearm roll is continued as before, it will be found that the portato has become a stopped stroke. The more we reduce the length covered by our eight quavers, the sharper becomes the separation. It should be noted that the down-bow version of this stroke is more effective if the hand is turned in an exaggerated form of the down-bow hand-shape (Diagram 21, p. 41). The resultant movement can no longer be described as a forearm roll, being rather a small up and down movement of the wrist in the plane of the stroke, but the sound of this type of down-bow staccato is very close to that of the up-bow forearm roll staccato, and the speed is equally controllable. In both up- and down-bow versions it will be found helpful to exaggerate the respective hand-shapes as the speed is increased.

102

The second variety of staccato I recommend is a development of the movement studied in Exercises 25 and 26 of this lesson. There is no conscious forearm roll in this type which, in slow-motion, consists of a détaché movement in the main direction, punctuated by an almost imperceptible movement, with loosened hold, in the opposing direction.

Although in practice this return movement is reduced to being no more than a feeling of release between impulses in the slower staccato, and is not felt at all in the faster stroke, it does appear to be the key to this variety of staccato, and as such it is helpful to practise it as follows:

1. Play a group of four triplet figures, starting at the tip and progressing up the bow to the heel, so that you start the second group at the heel and progress back to the tip with the hand in an exaggerated down-bow shape.

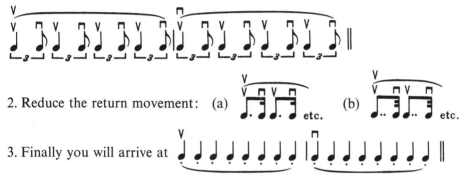

2. Reduce the return movement:

3. Finally you will arrive at

The speed is increased by reducing the size of the movement. It is a characteristic of this variety of staccato that it can be performed throughout the length of the bow, although we should note that in approaching the heel on an up-bow, the elbow needs to be pulled inward so that the tip of the bow swivels away from the player, and that, in starting down-bow right at the heel, the opposite adjustment becomes necessary (pushing the elbow forward so that the tip swivels towards the player). In the down-bow variety at speed it helps to exaggerate the down-bow shape of the hand to the point of playing on the inside edge of the hairs.

Relaxing after Staccato

EXERCISE 45

To relax after the staccato exercises, do two-string or three-string crossing exercises in even groups of notes, first in whole bows and later in sub-divisions. Forget about the detail of thumb positions, etc., but remain completely soft in all joints of fingers, wrist and arm. Concentrate on the stroke as if it were gently undulating on one string, with more wrist and less finger motion.

In all our exercises we have developed the flexibility and the firmness of the fingers, the four fingers and thumb usually on the bow. It must be remembered, however, that those with short arms or short fingers may find these exercises induce tension in the upper half of the bow, especially in the down-bow. The third and fourth fingers are not essential when the bow is lying on the string in the upper half in the down-bow.

In fact it is a good idea to alternate these exercises with long strokes, both fast and slow on one string and on the waving of two or more strings, holding the bow with only the thumb and first finger. This will release the arm and induce the flexibility and suppleness of wrist movement. It will also increase the strength and responsibility of the second finger when done with both first and second fingers. Even at the nut, the second may develop sufficient flexibility and strength to help balance the bow in motion.

The Tremolo

The practice of this stroke, as of the staccato, too often leads to unwanted 'seizures'. This is the result of regarding such rapid movement as a straightforward pull and push, which leads to the building up of tensions in the opposing muscles until one arrives at a state of spasm. I would propose instead regarding tremolo as an oscillation – that is, the smallest wave motion derived from our 'pendel' and pivot movements – which allows both speed and firmness combined with flexibility.

Practise tremolo first in the upper quarter of the bow, then in the middle and finally at the nut.

Exercises on the bow, using only the first and second fingers with the thumb

These are important, and I would encourage students to follow them, in order to develop maximum wrist flexibility, and also to develop the second finger to its maximum capacity. This can, to a certain extent, take over the function of the third and fourth fingers:

(a) In balancing the bow;

(b) In replacing the fourth finger in a down-bow crescendo and in replacing the third finger in an up-bow crescendo.

Cultivate an awareness of the special function of the 'circle' between thumb and second finger in acting as a pivot on two planes: (1) the horizontal, which allows the compensating movement that keeps the bow parallel with the bridge to happen partially within the hand (thus cutting down on the extent of compensation from wrist, arm and sometimes shoulder); and (2) the vertical, which allows crossing between two adjacent strings to occur within the fingers without changing level of wrist or arm.

To achieve this awareness it is worth practising with the circle hold alone. Start by placing the middle of the bow on the string with a normal hold. Then take off all the fingers except the second and the thumb, and draw the bow to the tip and back again to the middle. Do not put pressure on this hold as it can easily cause strain.

Repeat this a few times on each string. Then, starting at the middle, place the fourth finger on the bow and make an up-bow stroke to the heel, feeling the compensating movement which takes place around the circle and the fourth finger balancing the increased weight towards the heel. Repeat this a few times on each string. Then try some string-crossing exercises at the heel with this hold (thumb, second and fourth fingers), gradually adding the other fingers in such a way that they allow the crossing movement to continue unimpeded. Feel the degrees of responsibility in each finger during these exercises.

If the speed of the stroke in the lower half is increased slightly, it will soon be found possible to leave off the fourth finger without producing a crescendo and eventually to lift the bow off the string altogether and replace it with the circle hold alone. It should be stressed, however, that this is to be achieved by balance and momentum only and not by gripping.

These exercises with the circle hold in the lower half are an effective antidote to excess tilting of the bow hairs when approaching the heel, a habit due to one or both of the following reasons: (1) Failure of the compensating movement in the fingers caused by stiffness, more often than not by a blocked thumb. This throws the responsibility for keeping the bow parallel wholly on to the wrist which, bending in its horizontal plane only, soon reaches its limit of movement and so is forced to tilt in order to enlarge its possibility of turning; (2) The common feeling that this tilting is the only way to compensate for the increasing weight towards the heel and consequently to avoid unwanted crescendi.

With regard to the second reason, while it should be admitted that this special tilting is an effective way of taking up the weight, it also produces a change of tone-colour which no sensitive ear can fail to detect. Furthermore it produces a position at the heel which hinders string-crossing movements within the hand and is inimical to strong accents, triple-stoppings on repeated down-bows, etc. These remarks do not apply to *pp* transparent whole-bow strokes in which the degree of tilt is equal throughout the bow length and which do not call for agility or power at the heel.

In the upper half of the bow, without the third or fourth finger down on the stick, the second finger can take over their function and actually achieve a crescendo either by pulling the stick inwards, or by pressing the stick outwards; using the third and fourth finger merely increases our control and hold over the bow and the power behind it, but not the flexibility.

Now we apply our work without third and fourth fingers to our early exercises in our genealogy of bowing strokes. In Exercise 9 when you lift the bow off the string, drop the third and fourth fingers on to the bow and take them off during every played note. This will also increase the relaxation and the speed of dotted rhythms. Apply our work with only the first and second fingers on the bow also to the exercises for playing sustained notes and to the three string exercises, the series beginning with Exercise 39. These exercises should not be done until the third and fourth fingers have been fully developed and until the second finger has been developed in its dual capacity, i.e. both in its vertical and in its horizontal functions. On G string retakes without the third and fourth fingers on the bow, the second finger finds it particularly difficult to balance the bow. There the third and fourth fingers can gather together touching the second finger, and be placed lightly on the bow in soft support.

For fast up-bow retakes, such as those in the Mendelssohn Concerto, it is a positive advantage to play without the third and fourth fingers on the stick, since wrist flexibility and speed are greatly enhanced. Here the second finger extends down the stick somewhat beyond its normal position, so as to take over the function of the third finger and lift the bow off the string. In the Mendelssohn the very first lift is helped by the third and fourth fingers, which are then raised clear of the stick. Care must be taken, however, to cushion the landing on the soft down-bow.

When working on spiccato in this way take the fingers off when the bow lands on the note and continue the same stroke; put them on again as the bow is lifted. Keep them on as you change direction, lifting them off when the bow touches the string in the opposite direction, say in the up-bow, putting them on as you lift the bow still in the up-bow direction, keeping them on as you change back to down-bow, and taking them off as the down-bow touches the string again.

Another interesting exercise, which is complementary to those for the thumb and two fingers, is to make a pianissimo up-bow, and to let the bow lie, as it were, inside the first finger and balanced by the third and fourth fingers. Taking the thumb away, you will find it is perfectly possible for the bow at a 45° angle, lying on the side of the hairs, to be carried inside the bent first finger and balanced with the fourth. This releases the thumb. It is a good exercise because it is important in the up-bow when we approach the nut for the thumb muscle to soften.

Compensatory exercises

In this lesson we have considered various extreme positions and movements, particularly those of the hand. In actual playing, however, we must never go to the extreme of any particular movement, but always be conscious of its centre so as not to lose sight of its essential function. This is an important principle that applies to all aspects of violin technique.

Yet it is valuable as an exercise to experiment with certain grossly exaggerated positions; such exercises I call 'Compensatory Exercises'. As we have discovered, no one position or movement is correct in each and every similar circumstance. The value of these exercises lies in the experience of what is nominally wrong, so that we can perceive more clearly the correct solutions to the technical problems that occur.

1. Practise with the violin (a) pointing almost vertically up, (b) pointing almost vertically down, (c) rotated to the extreme left, and (d) rotated to the extreme right. Observe how the right hand fingers adjust to keep the bow from falling towards or away from the bridge in (a) and (b), and the action of the right arm in (c) and (d).
2. Practise up-bows in the following four ways:
   (a) Without allowing the wrist to bend. For the bow to be kept straight, the shoulder must be pushed back and down. Notice how the shoulder controls the movement of the bow during the stroke.
   (b) With the wrist very bent. The shoulder begins in a forward position (elbow down) and must be continually adjusted during the stroke.
   (c) With the elbow very high. The shoulder begins in a high forward position; the wrist is depressed and the lack of flexibility in the fingers causes a compensatory adjustment in the angle of the hand throughout the stroke.
   (d) With the elbow very low (cp. the old-fashioned practice of holding a book between the elbow and the side of the body). Finger flexibility is all important to keep the bow straight.
3. Practise down-bows in the same four ways and observe the different compensating reactions of wrist, elbow, shoulder, etc. In (a), where the wrist remains unbent, allow the bow to travel 'round the corner', out of parallel with the bridge, on its approach to the point. This obliges the forearm to open completely, reducing the play in the shoulder, and provides a type of quiet strength at the point which may occasionally be found useful in performance.

LESSON V

Left-Hand Movements

The same technical principles will apply to the left hand as to the right. The three main functions of fingerfall, shifting and vibrato will be seen to be not only related, but to proceed from a waving action, varying in amplitude from a narrow vibration to a broad sweep. The lateral movements in left-hand pizzicato are also incorporated in this system.

The fingers, of course, have special tasks for which they must be highly trained. This training consists in developing elasticity of stretch and spring – as of a rubber band and a coil spring – from the elongated to the compressed or folded as well as from the folded to the elongated, in three pairs of directions on three different planes: the horizontal, the vertical, and the lateral. Incidentally, the analogy of the rubber band and coil spring is not accurate, because the same finger can act like either, and further, far from providing an automatic invariable response as these do, can remain relaxed in either elongated or folded position (or anywhere in between), and is able at any moment to apply the power of either stretch or spring through a controlled act of will.

You can try inventing exercises with rubber bands and with rubber balls to increase both stretch and squeeze between thumb and fingers.

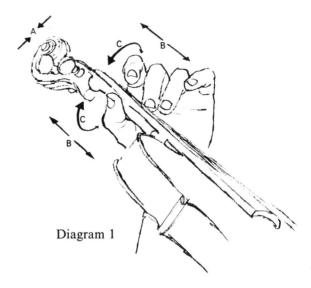

Diagram 1

108

We must train each finger separately on each of three planes, as well as develop the response between thumb and finger or fingers – a relationship of opposition – also on three planes: (A) face-to-face, i.e. finger-tip to thumb-tip as when pressure is applied and resisted diagonally, almost vertically through fingerboard and neck; (B) horizontally – in opposing directions along strings and fingerboard; (C) laterally, as in left-hand pizzicato – see Diagram 1 opposite. Exercising the hand in this manner in various positions on the fingerboard and combining it with the propelling power of the arm and body, we shall have control over the whole extent of the fingerboard.

These exercises all overlap and, although we are concentrating on one aspect at a time, we cannot overlook all the others, which are always associated more or less actively. Let us first consider the three planes before playing any exercises.

Horizontal movements

WAVE MOTION

Hold the left hand in the playing position, without the instrument, with loose wrist, palm facing you, and wave it as if saying goodbye to yourself. Do this a long time.

See that the wrist and fingers are completely soft, offering no resistance. Now induce a passive waving of the hand by moving your forearm back and forth (Diagram 2). To introduce a circular swing into the continuing waving of the hand, add a sideways oscillation of the elbow and arm (Diagram 3). Now make as big

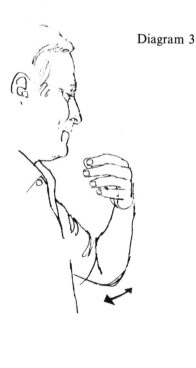

Diagram 3

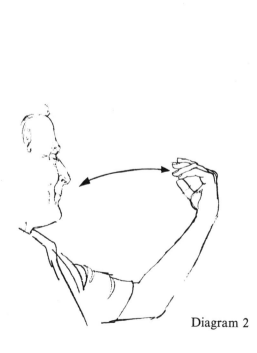

Diagram 2

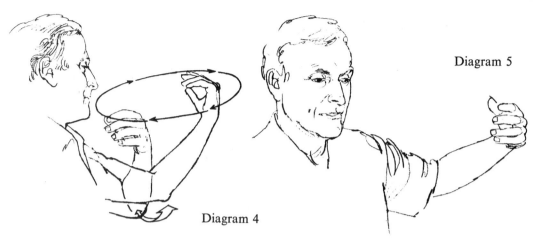

Diagram 5

Diagram 4

circles in the air as you can (Diagram 4). If you take the position of looking down upon the circle, the hand must appear to move in a clockwise direction. See that the circle is on a single horizontal plane. If anything, the plane should *rise* away from you and not fall away from you. To achieve this very wide perfect circle, you must increase both the opening and the closing of the forearm against the upper arm and the sideways swing of the elbow and upper arm to and from the body. While doing this great circular movement, do not allow the neck and shoulder to stiffen; soften them so that the head and shoulder join in sympathetically or at least do not resist.

Now, continuing this circular movement, apply one impetus on each complete wave: first on *each outward* movement of the forearm, as if you were going to smack a wall in front of you with the back of your hand (Diagram 5); and secondly on *each inward* movement of the forearm, as if you were smacking your chin (Diagram 6).

If you study these movements you will notice that at the moment you are smacking

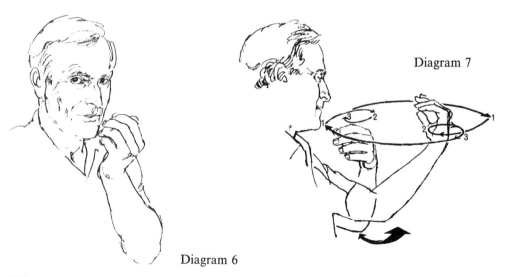

Diagram 7

Diagram 6

the wall the elbow has already begun to swing or 'pendel' towards your body and the moment you are slapping or smacking your chin, the elbow is well on its way out.

In thinking of your fingers during the smacks, imagine that in hitting the wall in front of you, you are doing so with your knuckles while the finger-tips and thumb touch each other momentarily, having elongated during the outward journey, and that conversely, when slapping yourself, you do so momentarily with open palm and fingers.

Now instead of applying your smack repeatedly on the wall or your chin once every complete wave, alternate between them so that in three complete waves you once hit the wall and once hit yourself. If you count three – one, two, three; one, two, three . . . etc. – on the first 'one', your open palm or, preferably, the outside of your finger-nails (folded fingers) will hit your chin, and on the second 'one' the back of your hand will hit the wall (Diagram 7 opposite).

This movement in the left hand corresponds to the elongated and folded states of the right hand in alternate up- and down-bows.

STRENGTHENING THE FINGERS

Now let us go back to the preliminary exercises for strengthening the fingers, this time on the violin, before combining the finger action with the motive power of the 'wave'.

Taking up the violin in the playing position, place the second finger on the A string about half-way along the neck of the violin. Press the finger down against the thumb's resistance on the side of the neck. See that the hand is in a good relaxed 'middle' position, fingers and thumb separate and rounded, plenty of space within the hand, the forearm light and soft, ready if pushed to 'pendel' freely (Diagram 8).

Now with the forearm try to pull the violin away from your chin-collarbone hold. Allow the wrist to be drawn out *away* from you. Allow the fingers, including the second finger, which is holding down the note on the A string, and the thumb, to elongate passively as they are being pulled out away from you. At their maximum elongation they have to oppose any increasing tug of the forearm by holding on to string and neck (with finger and thumb pads) even more tightly (Diagram 9). While

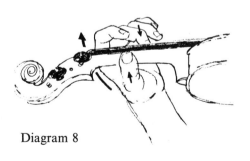

Diagram 8

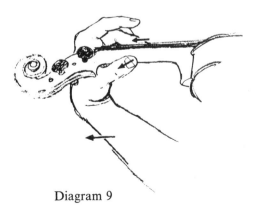

Diagram 9

111

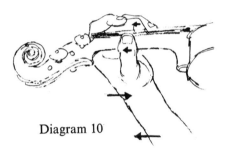

Diagram 10

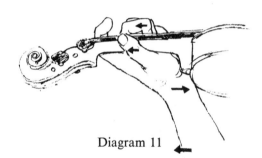

Diagram 11

maintaining the tug of the forearm away from you, pull the wrist in towards you so that the finger and thumb draw themselves back to their normal playing position (Diagram 10).

The finger and thumb can exert themselves even beyond this point and pull themselves together with the wrist into their tightly folded state – still always against the contrary drag of the forearm (Diagram 11). As soon as this finger and wrist activity is relaxed, the forearm will win its way and finger and wrist will automatically be drawn into their elongated and protruding states.

This exercise should be done with each finger – the order of fingers being 2, 4, 3 and 1 – on each of the four strings – A, D, E and G, in that order. While the arm is trying to pull the violin away, the head is allowed to drop its weight (only partly) on to the chin-rest and gently pulls back to maintain a grip on the violin against the collarbone. Always avoid touching the neck of the violin with the base of the first finger – in any case it must never lean on the neck and the neck must never be clamped between the base of the first finger and the thumb. When shifting from an upper to a lower position on a down-bow, with the left arm moving to the right, the base of the first finger will not touch the neck as the hand 'rises' to the first position. On the left-ward swing of the left arm, as in an up-bow, the base of the first finger will brush the neck as the hand 'falls' to first position. When the violin is played on open strings, or on a trill on open strings so that during the intervals between the fingered notes there is no finger on any string, it is quite in order to allow the base of the first finger to lend gentle support.

In the following exercise, in which the violin is pushed into the neck, the head should be raised slightly, and the neck should be completely relaxed. Again starting in the 'middle' position (Diagram 12), we allow our fingers and wrist to accept the forearm push and fold upon themselves. As this push is increased, they must offer increased resistance not to be pushed away from the note that the finger and thumb are holding. Further increased resistance against the arm push takes the form of the finger pushing itself determinedly into the middle position (Diagram 13) and even further into an elongated state (Diagram 14). As soon as the finger resistance is relaxed, the continuing arm push takes over and the finger snaps back into its folded state. Do this exercise with all four fingers individually on all four strings, in the same order as in the preceding exercise.

112

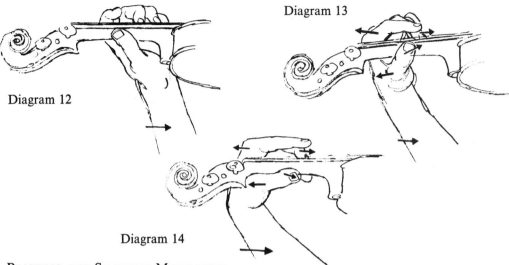

Diagram 13

Diagram 12

Diagram 14

PINCHING AND SNAPPING MOVEMENTS

Now let us combine our new resistance and strength in the fingers with our wave motion, at first without the violin.

Imagine you had a very, very long nose like Pinocchio, and that you wanted to pull it out even longer. You remember that I asked you before to hit the wall in front of you with your knuckles, while the elongated fingers touched each other. Now, instead of hitting the wall on each wave, imagine you are pinching that nose of yours, pulling it out a little each time and simultaneously snapping the fingers into the folded position. In the other direction, instead of only hitting your chin with your nails, at that very moment snap your folded fingers into their elongated position, as if jumping off the chin (Diagram 16).

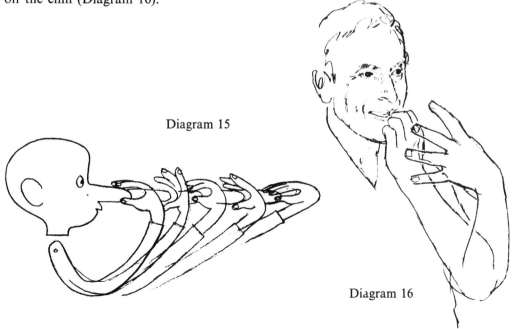

Diagram 15

Diagram 16

If we think in circles, the pulling out (pinching) will be the farther part of a clock-wise circle, and the snapping will be the nearer part of this circle, the fingers actively pulling the hand back. In a shift to a lower position on the violin the farther part of the circle (the elongation of the fingers while the tip of the finger and the thumb 'pinch' the note) will be longer and more pronounced than the nearer part of the circle. In a shift to an upper position the snapping motion, launching the hand towards the bridge (the nearer part of the circle), will cover a long distance and will be more pronounced than the elongation (the farther part of the circle).

Making these circles, we can stress the pinching and relax on the nearer part of the circle. This gives us a one-two, one-two movement. Using this pinching movement, we can shift down and up the fingerboard as described in the last paragraph. We can also stress the nearer part of the circle in a one-two, one-two movement; that is the snapping action to move up and down the fingerboard. In both cases there must be complete relaxation on 'two', the unstressed half of the movement.

It is also useful to practise these circles in triplet rhythm, so that the stress or accent alternates between the pinch and the snap. This can be practised in two ways: (a) the finger slides on the string, its maximum pressure occurring at opposite ends of the movement, pinching on the lower note and snapping on the upper note; (b) the finger remains on one note. In both cases, however, the finger should relax between the alternate moments of pressure. The children at my school call their pinching and snapping locomotion 'caterpillar' and 'catapult' respectively.

The description of shifting in terms of caterpillar and catapult action represents a description of exercises to develop recoil, elasticity, spring, etc. But when finally we shift in performance we combine these movements in a wave motion, containing both the pivotal displacement and the whole carried forearm displacement, in which sometimes the one and sometimes the other is dominant. This depends on the bow stroke, its reaction in the body and the distance to be travelled. We will go into this in greater detail when we consider the co-ordination of the two hands in Lesson VI.

As I said in the Introduction, having analysed and practised individual movements in great detail, we finally digest and absorb them until they become one smooth, composite and almost subconscious wave. We gradually lose and forget the theoretical scaffolding. This is of course the ideal state, provided always that we can return to repair our technical structure whenever it needs it – which is almost every day. For this we require our analytical foundation.

Vertical movements

These will bring a welcome quietness after all the energetic waving we have done. We have already made the acquaintance of this action in Lesson III. You may remember how we raised the weight of the left arm on each finger in turn, bringing the knuckles to their highest elevation.

Play a C major scale of two octaves over the four strings, beginning with the second finger on C in the second position on the G string. Raise the hand energetically on each finger, releasing the thumb to bend in sympathy, and between each finger effort straighten the thumb, bringing the knuckles down and releasing tension in the finger correspondingly (see Lesson III, Diagrams 10 and 11, p. 58).

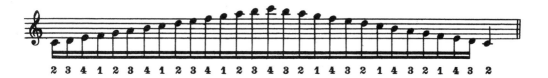

Now hold all the fingers down on one string or one on each string:

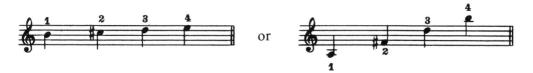

Lift them singly and in pairs – 2 and 4, 1 and 3 – first into a bent position (Diagram 17a), then straightening them out as high in the air as possible (b). For this exercise to be effective, the fingers must be raised like lightning – as quickly and as energetically as possible. Remember that the 'lift' is as important as the fall. Try alternating a quick up and long down position with a quick down and long up position.

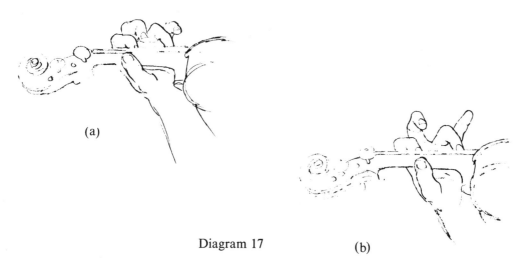

(a)

Diagram 17   (b)

Now co-ordinate each raising of the
fingers with an in-going movement
of the wrist.

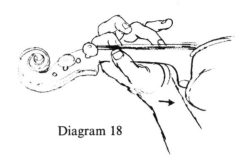

Diagram 18

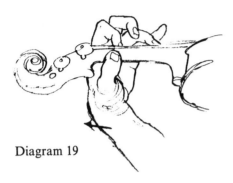

Diagram 19

Now co-ordinate each raising of the
fingers with a protruding movement
of the wrist.

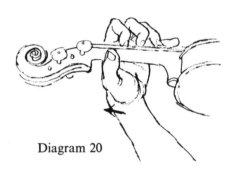

Diagram 20

Now co-ordinate each falling of the
fingers with a protruding movement
of the wrist.

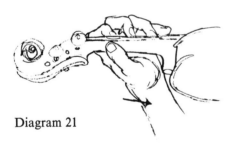

Diagram 21

Now co-ordinate each falling of the
fingers with an in-going movement
of the wrist.

The snap of the lifting finger is as important as the resilient hammer of the falling finger. It helps enormously in the distinctness and articulation of descending scales.

We now return to the two-octave C major scale in the second position. Notice that the left arm and elbow must be free to 'pendel' in order to facilitate the passage over the four strings; the movement is from right to left in the ascent and from left to right in the descent, so that on the G string (Diagram 22) the arm is further across the body than on the E string (Diagram 23). There should also be a small 'pendel' to the right each time the fourth finger comes down, to enable it to stop the string easily while maintaining its rounded position.

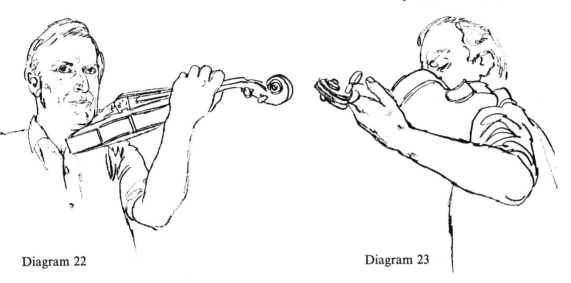

Diagram 22   Diagram 23

Further horizontal movements

The following exercises will assist chromatic fingering, where the movement of the fingers is continuous along the strings in a horizontal direction.

1. Place the second finger on the D string at a point half-way up the neck of the violin, and move it backwards and forwards from the extreme folded to the extreme elongated position. The other fingers should rest lightly on another string or other strings, or be held just above the strings, relaxed and in a rounded position. The thumb rolls horizontally on the neck of the violin in the opposite direction to the finger, sensing a continuous push and pull even while remaining on one spot.

   Do this with each finger in turn (2, 4, 1 and 3) on each of the four strings (D, A, G and E), keeping the hand half-way up the neck of the violin. At no time should the base of the first finger touch the fingerboard or neck.

2. Now with the fingers lightly resting on the string or strings, stroke the neck of the violin horizontally with the thumb to its maximum extension in both directions.

3. Now do the first series of exercises moving the thumb with each finger movement in the opposite direction, gently stroking the violin neck.

4. (a) Now combine the last exercise with an in-going movement of the wrist on each complete movement.

   (b) Now combine the same exercise with an out-going or protruding movement of the wrist on each complete finger-thumb movement.

   A further left-hand exercise is to leave fingers and thumb on one spot, while all the time making a maximum movement in the wrist and fingers, correlated with the elbow, etc. Maintain an even pressure during the whole period of the swing. The

117

complementary exercise is the training of the fingers independently of the whole arm-swing. In this exercise we move the fingers singly from a folded to an extended position, co-ordinated only with a wrist movement without arm-swing.

Finally do Exercises 4 (a) and (b) again, but instead of the thumb stroking the neck, let it roll slightly on one spot exerting pressure in opposition to the finger, sometimes in one horizontal direction, sometimes in the other. Now, holding one finger on the fingerboard on a note, co-ordinate several wrist waves with one staggered elongation of another finger and again with one staggered folding of the same finger. In other words, with each smaller wrist wave, the finger moves a semitone up or down the fingerboard (the hand as such still remaining in one place in relation to the instrument's neck). You will find that in this co-ordination the wrist helps 'throw' the finger either way. Do this exercise between pairs of fingers – 1 and 2, 2 and 3, 3 and 4; 1 and 3, 2 and 4, 1 and 4.

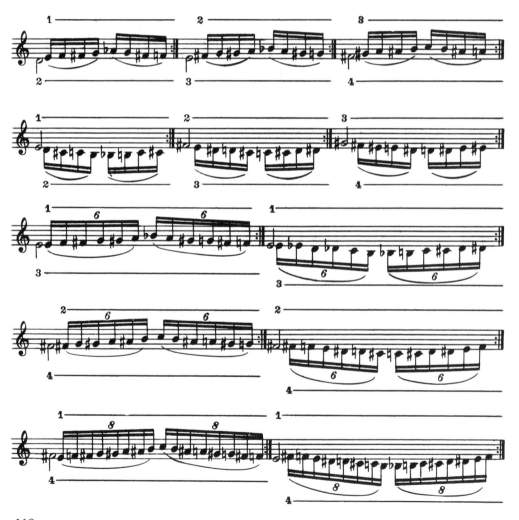

Left-hand Movements

Lateral movement – left-hand pizzicato

Against the resistance of the thumb, press the tip of each finger (the order should be 2, 4, 1 and 3) firmly on to the string so that the first joint gives way (see Diagram 24, Lesson III). Pull the string sideways with the finger-tip. Finally, the string refuses to be pulled any further and jumps back, as you pluck it, pulling the finger away and up. The left-hand pizzicato becomes more difficult (a) as the distance between held note and plucking finger lessens, and (b) when the fourth finger plucks. This fourth finger must be especially trained. Work with each finger on each string in first position, holding first, second or third finger on the note plucked.

Naturally the first finger can only pluck open strings as it can only pluck notes below it (unless it plucks a harmonic from below!). This also requires a special balancing act between first finger and thumb. Practise descending scales in the first position – *bow* 'picking' the top note on each string, either the third finger in first position when using open strings, or the fourth finger in all higher positions.

A related movement can greatly help the playing of fifths in higher positions. This technique consists of pulling the lower string over nearer to the higher (less often pushing the higher towards the lower), rolling over two strings, and preparing them with the help of the finger behind the playing finger; once the playing finger sits squarely on two strings intonation can be adjusted, without the risk of pushing the strings apart. This technique is useful not only in double stops, but in cantilena passages in which the interval of the fifth has to bridge smoothly upward over two strings without the playing finger losing its hold on the note.

Genealogy of exercises

Now let us finally return to our movements up and down the fingerboard, this time audibly.

You will see how by becoming aware of these elements – the waves and their alternating directions – we will always be ready to co-ordinate the left-hand movement with the right-hand stroke and its resultant body-swing. Usually because of the greater amplitude of the right-hand movement in comparison with that of the left arm, which is more concerned with stopping the notes on the strings, it is the right arm which dominates the sympathetic swing of the body and therefore also the left-arm elbow swing to a certain extent.

It is obvious that we must be able to shift in both directions on both up- and down-bows. At the same time there is a definite tendency for the left arm to swing to the right on a down-bow and to the left on an up-bow. Let us train these two directions separately, starting with the rightward swing.

The left elbow swings to the right. The hand goes into its elongated position with protruding wrist, knuckles raised and shoulder falling backwards. This might be visualized as a pivot movement with the fulcrum roughly at the mid-point between wrist and elbow. In practice, however, the fulcrum is more nearly at the finger-tip and thumb, especially if the finger is travelling while the thumb stays in one position.

In this latter exercise the finger is thrown to the lower position each time the elbow 'pendels' to the right.

By its very nature the complementary movement, i.e. going from a lower to higher position on a rightward swing of the elbow, will cover a longer distance, as the whole hand is both carried and thrown by the elbow 'pendel' to the right. In this case the pivot is really in the shoulder.

In the up-bow the tendency of the left elbow is to swing to the left. Here again the shift from a lower to an upper position occurs in a pivoting motion, the fulcrum being more nearly in the thumb. The shifting from a higher to a lower position is a carried movement, the whole arm opening as the elbow swings slightly to the left.

These four movements can each be correlated with the pulling and pushing of the fingers into elongated and folded positions respectively, as with the throwing of the fingers into elongated and folded positions.

This will all become evident in Lesson VI. Suffice it now to say that the left elbow 'pendel' occurs naturally as the arm hangs loosely from the shoulder when the upper body swings slightly. It will be noticed that it 'meets' the body; as the body rotates anti-clockwise (as seen from above) the elbow comes closer and vice versa. As an experiment, try moving arm and body as one piece – now you know what it really means to be 'petrified'!

FIRST SERIES OF EXERCISES

With each finger in order (2, 4, 3 and 1) and on each string in order (D, G, E and A), slide in triplet rhythms as widely as possible. Allow the thumb to travel along naturally.

In the next exercises do not worry about accurate intonation. This will come naturally when the movements become soft and easy and the ear can dictate to sensitive, strong and flexible fingers and limbs. The notes which I indicate are at first merely to serve as a guide to the approximate amplitude of the wave.

Beginning with the D string, work your way up in broken thirds and back down again.

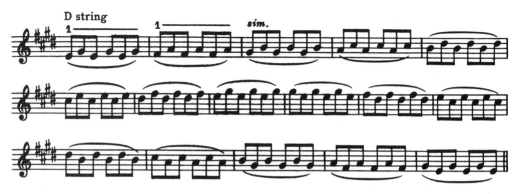

Work your way to wider intervals until you slide easily over two octaves on the G string with a single finger. To do this, you use the great wave action described in the earlier part of this lesson which we worked on without violin. Those with small hands may find that they cannot quite jump this distance. They should try to come as near as they can.

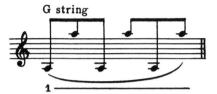 

Do these exercises again, this time beginning on the upper note.

You will notice that you will be able to do the small distances almost entirely on a forearm metronome movement. The larger movements will need a broader carrying swing of the upper arm and elbow. As we saw earlier, you can thus initiate the same movement in two ways, a great convenience when co-ordinating with the right hand. Remember this fact.

Next play broken thirds with two fingers, two octaves up and down.

These should be played on each string with our three pairs of fingers: 1 and 2, 2 and 3, 3 and 4.

When the left hand shifts to a lower position, whether by an inward or by an outward elbow-swing, the chin always pulls a little on the chin-rest. Be careful to keep the neck relaxed, particularly on each upward shift. Remember to keep the wrist soft and the hand high. Take care also not to develop a stiffening of the right arm while you are concentrating on the movements of the left.

SECOND SERIES OF EXERCISES
In this series we again play broken thirds, fourths, etc. Begin in the lower positions and move the finger or fingers in a wave action, involving the hand, but letting the thumb continue to touch the same spot on the neck with its pad.

THIRD SERIES OF EXERCISES
Here, we keep the finger on one note but move the thumb deliberately. (Remember it moves in the opposite direction to the one in which the finger *would* move, if it were moving!)

121

The Trill

The trill grows naturally out of our exercises in waves, the wave movement now becoming smaller and faster to resemble an oscillating pivot movement. Once the vertical movements of the fingers have been trained, we co-ordinate them with this pivot movement, which throws the trilling finger like the hammer of an electric bell. The necessary co-ordination can be developed in three stages:

(a) Holding one finger down on the string, start a backward-forward-backward roll; arrive on the trilling finger with the next forward roll – there is a small rotation of the forearm – and lift it with the next backward roll but one. Fingerfall is therefore combined with the pivot movement in the form of one and a half oscillations to each finger.

(b) Go straight from a backward roll on the holding finger to a forward roll on the trilling finger.

(c) To increase speed, simply reduce the amplitude of the movement. Try this with different combinations of fingers on each of the four strings.

Vibrato

Vibrato is the smallest movement in our series of waves. We can think of it as an oscillation deriving from the swing and pivot movements.

You must feel soft in all the joints and be aware of the vertical pressure on each finger in turn. This sensation should be cultivated on every note of every scale and arpeggio in every part of the fingerboard.

The difference between a wide and a narrow vibrato (and a violinist must command every width and every speed of vibrato) is regulated by the relative firmness or softness of the finger joints. When they are soft (though always rounded) they release and encourage a wider sweep in the wrist and arm. When they are firm they prevent this freer movement – the forearm vibrates more of a piece with the wrist though there must *always* remain some give, some elasticity in every joint, including wrist and fingers – and the movement is less of a swing than a pivot.

Artificial harmonics

To play an artificial harmonic, two fingers are required, one firmly holding a lower note which shortens the string, the other touching lightly a higher note – a spot corresponding to where a natural harmonic would be on the shortened string. Double harmonics occur when the first and second fingers stop two strings – shorten their vibrating length – and the third and fourth touch the exact divisions which produce the harmonics. The fingers must be supremely accurate. These harmonics sound most beautiful when played with vibrato.

Scales and arpeggios

To end this lesson we will practise scales and arpeggios with no waving, no vibrato at all, but with all joints soft and supple. The sound this produces is called 'white sound', which is very beautiful and effective in certain passages.

First play two-octave arpeggios, scales and chromatic scales on one string with one finger – each of the four fingers in turn on each of the four strings. In the ascent use either a swing movement, where the elbow leads with a swing to the right, or a pivot movement, where the elbow moves to the left.

Arpeggio on D string

Scale on G string

Chromatic scale on G string

Then do scales on one string with a pair of fingers. Follow this with scales with a group of three and of four fingers.

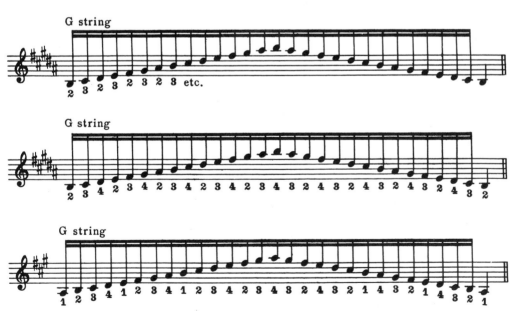

Lesson V

In practising scales on one string with fingerings 12 12, 123 123 or 1234 1234, it will be noticed, especially when practising slowly, that there is a subtle difference between the shifts on an up-bow and those on a down-bow. On the down-bow the shifts, whether up or down, always occur on an elbow-swing to the right. On an up-bow there is always some leftward tendency even when the shift is too long to be carried entirely by the pivot movements.

Then play chromatic scales with groups of two or more fingers, taking care to co-ordinate fingerfall and wave action.

G string

```
1  2  1  2 etc.
1  2  3  1  2  3
1  2  3  4  1  2  3  4
1  1  2  2  3  3  4  4  1  1  2  2 etc.
```

Finally play scales in thirds, sixths and octaves.

Scale in thirds on G & D strings

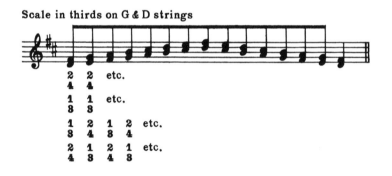

```
2  2     etc.
4  4
1  1     etc.
3  3
1  2  1  2 etc.
3  4  3  4
2  1  2  1 etc.
4  3  4  3
```

Scale in sixths on D & A strings

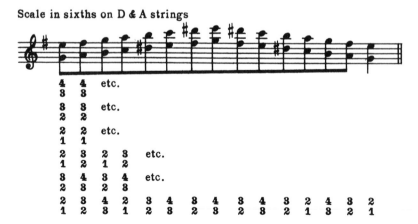

```
4  4        etc.
3  3
3  3        etc.
2  2
2  2        etc.
1  1
2  3  2  3  etc.
1  2  1  2
3  4  3  4  etc.
2  3  2  3
2  3  4  2  3  4  3  4  3  4  3  2  4  3  2
1  2  3  1  2  3  2  3  2  3  2  1  3  2  1
```

124

Scale in octaves on G & D strings

4 4 etc.
1 1

8 8 etc.
1 1

4 4 etc.
2 2

3 4 3 4 etc.
1 2 1 2

LESSON VI

Both Hands Together

Following on many broad hints in the course of the past five lessons about the integration of movements in the two arms, now finally we come to the fruits of our labours.

So far we have concentrated on the clarification and the development of movements in each limb separately, but one cannot think of violin playing until the separate functions of each arm become one function, one activity. Like love which requires two to become one, so violin playing only becomes alive with the complete integration and co-ordination of both hands. To achieve this state (in which the breathing also plays an essential part), the whole of the upper body must itself be flexibly, yet firmly poised, ready to yield to and to reconcile, as well as to initiate and maintain the movements. As we have seen, the right arm, when moving with energy and speed the full length of the bow from a folded to an extended position, is going to exert a greater influence on the body's capacity for adjusting to a shifting centre of gravity than the left arm exerts with its relatively reduced range of movement, the restricted 'pendel' of its angled elbow and its greater emphasis on individual finger action. Therefore the upper body in general accords with the right arm rather than with the left.

Try this. Stand on your toes, hold a stick in your right hand and swing it vigorously in large anti-clockwise circles in front and to the side of you. You will notice a small adjustment in your body as your chest turns horizontally anti-clockwise to counterbalance the outward throw of the right arm. Now this is obviously a crude example, but exaggerated as it is, it serves to illustrate the kind of reaction which becomes microscopic and subconscious in evolved violin playing. May I suggest that at this point you re-read Lesson I and do the various basic preparatory exercises in the light of Lessons II, III, IV and V.

Four basic patterns

The following exercises affect swing of body, balance on feet, etc.

EXERCISE 1

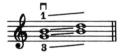

Both shoulders tend to move forwards. Left hand moves up the fingerboard towards the body, and right hand moves away from the body. Balance forward on your toes, pulling the spine backwards as the body makes a slow, longish swing.

126

EXERCISE 2

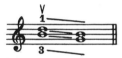

Both shoulders tend to move backwards. Left hand moves away from the body and right hand towards it. Balance with the chest forward and don't go too far back on the heels.

EXERCISE 3

Left shoulder moves forwards, right shoulder backwards. Left hand moves up the fingerboard, and right hand moves towards the body.

EXERCISE 4

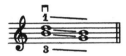

Left shoulder moves backwards, right shoulder forwards. Left hand moves down the fingerboard, and right hand moves away from the body.

Total co-ordination exercises – first series

These exercises are to be played at first at a medium level between the passive and the active. The bow is half lying on the string and half carried, allowing at all times an available margin for increase or decrease of pressure. Let pressure be applied from the release of the arm weight onto the stick, without disturbing the continuity of our medium level.

EXERCISE 1 (On one string)

Ex. 1a

Ex. 1b

Beginning with the down-bow exercise (Ex. 1a) we know that the stress on B flat will be part of the rightward 'pendel' of the left arm. Become aware of the slight rotation of the body which is co-ordinated with this 'pendel' and with the pressure of the right arm required for each accent. In the up-bow exercise (Ex. 1b) the same thing happens in the opposite direction.

Now do the first exercise (Ex. 1a) again, beginning with an up-bow, and observe the opposite rotation of the body, co-ordinated with the leftward 'pendel' of the

Lesson VI

left arm and with the accents. Follow this with the second exercise, beginning with a down-bow.

EXERCISE 2 (On two strings)

These exercises should be practised on two strings with the left-hand fingers stopping two notes, a whole tone apart. A change of position is required, not a stretch. Allow a slight rotation of the body on each stressed note in addition to the general body-swing associated with the down- and up-bow strokes.

This body rotation begins at the point of contact of the balls of the feet with the ground. The impulse from the right foot precedes the up-bow, pushing the floor to initiate the body rotation (Diagram 1); the left foot initiates the down-bow action (Diagram 2). (Of course in slow strokes this movement is reduced to very little or none, while in short strokes to the *opposite* directions only.) On continuous down- and up-bow strokes you will notice that the impulse occurs on the section of the stroke preceding the bow change (section C of the Basic Bow Stroke, p. 71). The bow change proper occurs when the impulse has travelled all the way from the ball of the foot to the bow, and while this impulse is covering this distance, the bow is still fulfilling its last length in the previous direction.

Of course this sensation is strongest in bowing which requires attack, distance and speed – and most obvious when playing on the G string where the bow is moving most horizontally.

EXERCISE 1 REPEATED

Let us now co-ordinate an outward pull of the left hand and wrist on each accented note in the down-bow Ex. 1a. If we examine the movements more closely, we find that the left shoulder moves slightly backwards, the left elbow pivots from left to right and the left wrist, protruding, elongates the fingers as it pulls towards the head of the violin.

Assuming the exercise is done around the middle of the bow, (1) right shoulder-blade moves down as long as the arm is bent and moves forward when the stroke is past the middle section; (2) right elbow and whole arm rotate inwardly; (3) knuckles and wrist depress in a slightly more pronounced way on each accented note than they would during the normal course of the down-bow.

In this particular combination of actions, therefore, the shoulders move in opposite directions and a slight rotation of the body occurs sympathetically as the right shoulder moves forwards and the left shoulder moves backwards.

The head oscillates as it puts more weight on the chin-rest and pulls slightly backwards on the stressed notes, or rather while the fingers (or a single finger) are being pulled.

128

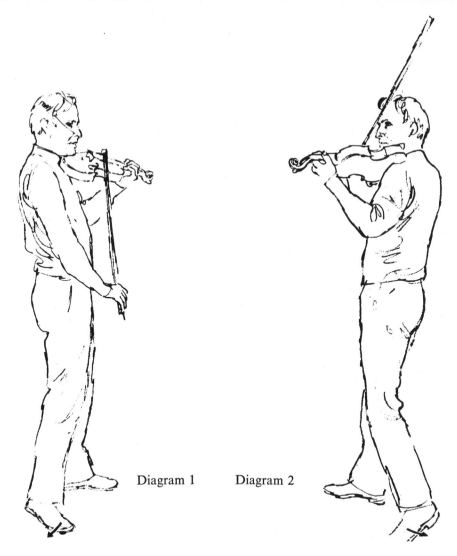

Diagram 1   Diagram 2

Between pulls the left-hand fingers should slightly release hold on the string, as they return to their first (normal) position. Here the left thumb remains in its position on the violin neck.

The opposite actions take place on the stressed notes in the up-bow Ex. 1b. The shoulders still move in opposite directions, but this time on the accented notes the right shoulder tends to move slightly backwards and the left slightly forwards, as the left-hand finger or fingers are pushed or folded in the direction of the bridge. Rotation of the body continues in the up-bow (five notes to a stroke), more pronounced during the accented notes, relaxing between the accents.

These exercises should be done until an absolutely smooth co-ordination of all elements becomes completely natural.

Inhalation and exhalation should occur respectively on every three or every five strokes. If strokes are slow and a breath must be taken on each, exhale on the down-bow and inhale on the up-bow. Begin the exhalation before the down-bow and the inhalation before the up-bow.

Lesson VI

EXERCISE 3 (On one string)

EXERCISE 4 (On two strings)

These exercises should be practised on two notes in all positions, with the fingers a third apart on two strings.

EXERCISE 3 REPEATED

On the accented notes the left hand moves in the direction of the violin bridge in the down-bows, and towards the head of the violin in the up-bows. Both shoulders move forwards on the down-bow accented notes and both move backwards on the up-bow accented notes. In these exercises the body hardly rotates; its action is rather a slight balancing forwards and backwards.

This means that the left elbow is describing more of a swing movement than a pivot movement, the wrist slightly in-bent in its own direction, the bow-stroke direction. I have therefore also given it a correspondingly greater distance to travel in this exercise, moving between 1st and 3rd positions instead of between 1st and 2nd, for instance.

This is a pleasant action – corresponding to the swinging of both arms in the same circle or in the same ellipse.

As I have said, both shoulders move slightly forward on the down-bow accented notes. The resulting body oscillation (backwards and forwards) reacts to the combined sympathetic action of the two limbs. Also on the down-bow accented notes (and the approach to them) the head releases its slight, lightly weighted grip on the chin-rest. The opposite simultaneous series of events occurs on the up-bow accented notes.

Basically this whole body co-ordination occurs on every note we draw and play and must therefore be practised on the basic movements of vibrato and shifting as on the various bow styles.

Alternate Exercise 1 with Exercise 3. Then try the following exercise, using fingers 2 and 4 in the lower positions with fingers 1 and 3 in the upper positions.

130

Total co-ordination exercises – second series

The essential difference between these and Exercises 1 and 3 of the first series is that the down-bow begins on the lower string and the up-bow on the higher, so that the accented notes in the down-bow and up-bow occur during the opposite right-hand rotation.

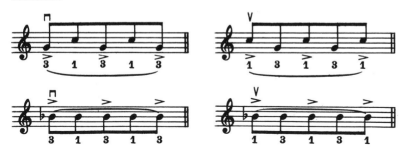

These co-ordinating exercises can be applied to every left-hand movement; for instance, to the left-hand thumb alone. Remember that when it moves backwards along the neck in the direction of the violin head, it corresponds to a finger shift to a higher note. Play Exercises 1 and 3 of the first series and all the second series exercises holding one note with the left hand and treating the thumb as we have treated each of the other fingers.

If we develop the left-hand action of finger versus thumb, it will allow the shifting to occur – particularly in high positions with the thumb against body-end of the violin neck, and in downwards shifts – without any effect on the player's (neck-collarbone-head) hold of the violin, the shift occurring through the interplay of fingers and thumb.

To this end the exercises co-ordinating the deliberate snap-out, snap-in finger action with the thumb exercises in opposite direction (if only of pressure) should be further co-ordinated with a left-arm throw (swing or 'pendel') in the direction of the fingers.

Total co-ordination exercises – third series

A further application of this co-ordination between left and right arms involving the body can be done on alternating solid and harmonic notes.

With an accent on the solid note, pull first towards head of violin on the down-bow and push towards bridge on the up-bow, then vice versa.

This is a useful exercise to give lightness to the hand while shifting. Never draw the bow 'flat', but imagine you are making the slight accent – whether in anti-clockwise rotation towards the higher sounding string on a down-bow and towards the lower sounding string on an up-bow, or vice versa. Even when changing strings (A string to D string, etc.), see that the bow is *carried*, at least partly, and *balanced* in the hand, without impinging on the softness, flexibility or adaptability of the wrist, hand or fingers.

Total co-ordination exercises with larger shifts

Our co-ordination can further be applied to larger left-hand shifts or slides. However before doing these total co-ordinating exercises with shifting I would like you to co-ordinate your stroke with a deliberate left-hand finger action. Just as you use the finger stroke in the right hand to increase the liveliness and initiative required for spiccato, sforzando and martelé and other bow strokes, you can co-ordinate the two hands as we have been doing in the last exercises, using a deliberate finger movement in the left hand, which like a Jack-in-the-box sends the finger from the folded to the extended position through the action of the finger itself. This action is an essential ingredient of all long shifts.

Applying this principle to the left hand, let us make large shifts with one finger on one string. The finger actively leads from a folded position on the lower note to an extended position on the upper note.

The same principle must be applied to a quick movement of the finger from the extended back to the folded (i.e. from the higher note to the lower). We must never forget that each movement in violin playing involves many others, even if they only appear as a trace. Now co-ordinate these with the right hand in the same way as we applied the left-hand directional pulls and pushes to the pivoting or swinging of the left elbow, in conjunction with bow stroke and body rotation.

Having done these jerky finger movements, we must again counteract them with their antidote – the pulling and pushing of the passive left-hand fingers. This sequence corresponds to the smooth détaché bowing exercises with minimum finger and maximum arm movement in the right hand (Exercises 11 and 12, p. 88).

By practising these two extreme forms of movement every day, we will control in the right hand every degree of bowing from détaché to martelé to spiccato, and in the left hand every kind of slide and shift – fast, slow or staggered like a dramatic bass or soprano, or like a chameleon's tongue able to strike out instantly and accurately for any note on the fingerboard.

132

EXERCISES ON TWO-OCTAVE JUMPS

Practise these first on the G string and later on every string.

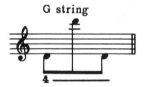

With the fourth finger beginning on D, slide to D two octaves higher on the G string; then do the same with the second and third fingers beginning on B and C respectively. Both hands travel roughly in the same direction, when the two-octave jump starts with a down-bow on the lower note. However, by using a whole *up-bow* while starting from the lower note, the hands meet on each top note. The body, as we have seen, describes less of a swing when the hands move towards each other or away from each other (i.e. from opposite directions) than when they move in the same direction.

Now do the same exercises beginning on the top note – i.e. with each finger and both up-bow and down-bow – and on various strings. Breathe once to each stroke.

Scales and arpeggios on one string

Practise scales with whole bows to each note and feel how with a very slow vibrato you can deliberately co-ordinate the downward and upward waves of vibrato with each stroke.

We have already seen how the finger can be affected in both directions with both swings of the elbow. But now we are allowing the body to be sympathetic to these movements.

This exercise can be done on broken thirds, arpeggios, chromatic scales, etc. I would suggest breathing once to every three strokes.

SHIFTING WITH ONE FINGER

Here is a useful list of scales and arpeggios, to be played with each finger separately on each of the four strings, and in a variety of different keys.

Major scale on D string

Melodic minor scale on G string

Harmonic minor scale on G string

Chromatic scale on G string

etc.

Arpeggio on D string

Broken thirds on D string

Play broken scales also in seconds, fourths, sixths, sevenths, octaves and tenths in different keys. Then try accenting alternate notes, keeping in mind the co-ordination between the left-hand accents, the pivot or swing movements of the left elbow and the other sympathetic body movements.

Broken scales with accents

etc.

Broken octaves are very useful – in two varieties:

Practise these both ascending and descending. Here, as each change involves a sizeable displacement whether up the fingerboard or down, it can coincide with an elbow movement, alternately pivot and swing.

These broken scales in seconds, thirds, fourths, etc. can also be played slowly, six or more notes to one stroke, one and a half shakes to each note (i.e. three movements to each note), the stress coming either on the pivot or the swing, depending on whether the left hand is moving in the same or in the opposite basic direction to the right hand. When working on these scales, take care to co-ordinate the movement of the body with the particular stress you have chosen.

Play two-octave arpeggios with one bow stroke for the full two octaves. Here, either the swing or the pivot predominates for each shift depending on whether down- or up-bow is used. In the pivoting examples the carrying movement is responsible for the total distance travelled and the pivot movement decreases in amplitude when the wrist is bent over the upper part of the violin.

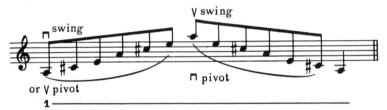

Of course, if you use two bows, the left elbow behaves thus:

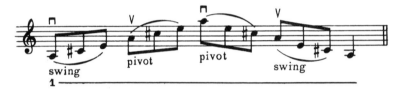

Do the same exercise beginning with an up-bow. You will begin with the pivot and the sequence will be reversed.

Follow up with some exercises on the various scales – chromatic, major, melodic and harmonic minor – and on double stops with one set of fingers, using the same bowing patterns.

SHIFTING WITH COMBINATIONS OF FINGERS

It should be no problem at this stage to grasp the timing of scales involving shifting, with two, three and four fingers.

Play a C major scale on the G string down-bow with first and second fingers alone, or with second and third, or with third and fourth fingers alone.

The shift occurs as in our one-finger arpeggio – on the swing with an inbound wrist – while the higher finger falls on an outbound, protruding wrist.

When you play the scale up-bow, the ascending shift still occurs on the inbound wrist, though this time it is on the pivot, not the swing, and the higher finger continues to fall on an outbound, protruding wrist.

In the descending scale down-bow, the shift on the higher finger occurs on the pivot with an outbound wrist (remember these movements are very small). In the descending scale up-bow the shift occurs on the swing and the same principle holds good.

To accentuate the co-ordination special exercises may be done moving the left thumb *alone* always in the opposite direction to the one the fingers take or would have taken, or even sliding fingers and thumb in opposite directions.

Trills and fingerfall

Practise fingerfall of trilling finger in both the outbound (protruding) wrist and inbound directions on both down- and up-bows. Don't forget the sympathetic body movements, even though they are now microscopic, and remember to keep the neck relaxed, the head upright.

Work on trills between groups of fingers, 1 and 2, 2 and 3, 3 and 4; 1 and 3, 2 and 4, 1 and 4; and in double stops. Paganini's sixth *Caprice* provides excellent examples of all these.

Practise fingerfall also on broken thirds – but in the following fingering, in the various positions: 1 3 2 4 1 3 2 4 upwards; 4 2 3 1 4 2 3 1 downwards.

Simple two-octave scales

After all these complex exercises, let us return to the simple two-octave scale in one position on four strings. Usually, this is where violin-playing begins, but I have deliberately left this co-ordination in scale playing to the last. Scales require such absolute evenness and such perfect co-ordination between vibrato and fingerfall. The well played scale is a test of all the co-ordinating exercises we have done until now. This is particularly evident in a downward scale when the new note is heard through the lifting of the higher finger. Unless the vibrato in the hand and the lifting are absolutely co-ordinated, this downward scale will never have the clarity and definition of the percussive upward scale.

Practise with fingerfall in both ways – i.e. in the two wrist directions. Actually, however, except for certain accepted patterns and in many fingered shiftings, fingerfall in one position will generally happen on the inbound wrist.

Bow co-ordination with string-crossing

Practise broken thirds, fourths, sixths, octaves and tenths on two strings.

Over 3 strings: G & A strings

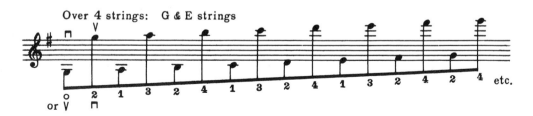

Over 4 strings: G & E strings

Remember that the exercises beginning down-bow on the lower string require great finger control in the right hand and precise right elbow timing and amplitude.

When beginning up-bow on the lower string, the right arm describes a considerably larger swing, which induces a larger left elbow swing in sympathy.

As I mentioned before, there are exceptions to all rules. Technically it is simply that another movement overrides the apparent one. For instance, in crossing over the four strings, using little bow and playing quickly, down-bow on the lowest and up-bow on the highest one, one stroke to each string, the displacement of the right arm is greater in the vertical plane than it is in the horizontal. Therefore, the vertical displacement over-rides the horizontal, with the result that the sympathetic swing of the left elbow is the opposite of that in the normal sympathetic down-bow swing. In other words, the left elbow swings to the left on the down-bow on the lower string, and the right on the up-bow on the upper string.

When doing down-bows and up-bows, two notes to a bow on two strings alternating, we are actually combining clockwise and anti-clockwise rotation in the one stroke.

In the first example the clockwise rotation involving the minimum arm movement occurs at the change of string, down-bow to up-bow, and the anti-clockwise at the change of string, up-bow to down-bow.

In the second example the anti-clockwise rotation involving the maximum arm movement occurs between a down-bow and an up-bow, and the minimum between an up-bow and a down-bow. Play the note preceding the change, thinking of the third section of our basic bow stroke – light and fast, and already belonging to the next stroke.

137

Total co-ordination in different styles of bowing

To co-ordinate the different styles of bowing with the movements of the body and of the left arm and fingers, we should apply the different left-hand patterns we have studied in Lessons V and VI to all the bowing exercises in Lesson IV.

*   *   *   *   *

In these six lessons we have reduced the technique of violin playing to basic waving patterns which leave no part of the body unco-ordinated. It must always be recalled, however, that we have been studying *means* – means which will make our ends more worthy, higher, more imaginative and ever closer to music's intention and purpose. Without these means, as violinists, our dreams remain useless and silent, or even worse than silent when audible! But when we can determine every subtlest inflection of accent, stress or volume, when we can alter speed, amplitude and energy of vibrato to suit every expressive need, we possess a palette beyond description.

APPENDIX I

Daily Practice and Warming-up Exercises

In the Introduction (p. 15) I suggested how this book can be used by teachers and students. I would here like to offer some hints on practising, and set out a series of exercises which aim to prepare the more advanced player within a short space of time for the successful performance of the main types of movement involved in violin playing.

Hints on practising

1. It is good to practise in both sitting and standing positions.

2. Be careful never to clench the jaw. If there is a tendency to stiffness, put down the violin and stretch the jaw (a) open, and (b) as far forward as possible.

3. Concentrate specifically on your breathing from time to time during practice. In this connection I can thoroughly recommend singing or humming either your own or another part while playing. Not only does it focus attention on breathing, but also – particularly when you sing another part – avoids excessive pre-occupation with the production of a single melodic line, and thus broadens the basis of musical concentration.

4. The continuous sound of the violin directly under the player's ear can be tiring and distracting over long periods. For prolonged, quiet yet concentrated practice I recommend use of a five-pronged iron or steel practice mute. Whereas a tight-gripping mute can affect the basic pattern of the violin's vibrations, the practice mute has a minimal carry-over effect, even when used for long periods, since it acts only by its weight and does not grip. It is a useful protective device both for the violinist himself and for those near him, particularly just before a concert.

5. Between every effort in your playing and during every pause, deliberately return to a state of relaxation and softness in all your joints. In time this will permeate even the act of performance itself.

6. Perhaps the most important principle to observe in practising is the precision and control of the maximum number of concurrent details. The mind must be continually active, checking detail after detail. Remember: the more perfect the practice, the more perfect the performance.

Appendix I

Warming-up exercises

These exercises are arranged under sub-headings describing the nature of the movement concerned. It is recommended that right and left hands should be exercised alternately, the proportion of the available time allotted to each depending on the individual player's needs.

PRELIMINARY

Make a selection of breathing, posture, stretching and waving exercises from Lesson I.

THE RIGHT HAND

1. *Flexibility*

Start with harmonics on two strings, slurred in groups of 5 and played without pressure in all parts of the bow; for example:

Then slur them in groups of 6, 4 and 2, and finally play single notes:

Follow this with a combined movement at the heel:

The right-hand fingers should here yield to the string-crossing movement rather than attempt to initiate it. This movement is easier to perform if the stick is not tilted too far from the player.

During the course of these exercises the left-hand pressure can be increased sufficiently for stopped notes to be produced with the minimum of effort.

2. *Pressure*

Practise the 'expanding circle' exercise as described in Lesson IV (pp. 77–78). Though the bow does not move across the string, the right hand should assume both down- and up-bow shapes, and the exercise should be tried at all parts of the bow on all the strings, with a gradual increase in the frequency of the squeezes. (This is an excellent preparation for staccato.) To test the effectiveness of the 'upward' relaxation of the shoulder, allow the bow occasionally to be lifted right off the strings when the pressure is released.

3. *Swing*

On each string do a few whole-bow swings, first up- then down-bow, followed by a curved recovery in the air as described in Lesson II (p. 44). Then practise the same movement on shorter strokes, half- and quarter-bows, etc., first up-bow starting at the tip, then down-bow starting at the heel. Increase the speed, and then experiment with different types of attack ranging from soft to sharply accented and produced (a) from out of the air, and (b) by pre-stroke pressure as in martelé. It is particularly important to be conscious of the muscular tone necessary for each type of attack *before* beginning the stroke.

Follow these swinging movements with dotted rhythms in different parts of the bow (see 'Smack-Bounce' movement, pp. 45–46).

4. *Bounce*

Work through the ricochet and spiccato exercises in Lesson IV (pp. 95–98), culminating in a light, smooth détaché in the lower half. Follow this by practice of the following rhythm on the string in different parts of the bow:

The semi-quavers are produced by the hand being thrown in the whip-like movement described on pp. 98–99.

5. *Large String-crossing Movements*

(a) On the spot at the tip, middle of the bow and heel as described on pp. 44 and 82–83.

(b) Détaché in both halves of the bow:

Allow the head to move freely from side to side during this movement.

6. *Grand Détaché*

Play scales with the following bowing:

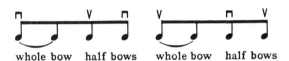

Appendix I

Then practise the following stroke, which combines the controlled pull of the

détaché with the élan of the swinging movement: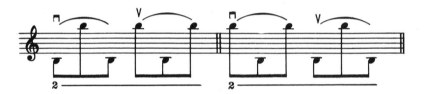

On the accented notes the arm moves more quickly, so that the hand is thrown into the shape of the following stroke in the opposite direction.

7. *Tremolo*
Practise the oscillating movement required for tremolo, described on p. 104.

8. *The Singing Tone*
Practise loud, slow, whole-bow notes in all left-hand positions, first singly and then on double stops. Cultivate a bow hold that allows the hand to feel the actual vibration of the string so that you can distinguish differences in pitch by means of their speed and amplitude.

THE LEFT HAND

1. *The Great Swing*
Practise two-octave shifts with one finger on one string, three notes to a bow:

These shifts should be done with each finger in turn (2, 4, 1, 3) on each string (D, E, G, A).

2. *Pull and Push on one Spot*
Place one finger down on a note and without leaving this note, pull the arm away from you towards the scroll of the violin and then push it inwards towards the bridge. Repeat this with each finger at different points along the strings. For weak fingers the variants described in Lesson V (pp. 111–12) with counter-effort from the finger should also be practised.

3. *Throw on one Spot*
With the finger remaining down on one note, produce a large vibrato movement from the wrist, combined with both a pull and push movement from the arm and an elbow-swing. Repeat this with each finger at different points along the strings.

4. *Finger Throw*
With the thumb remaining on one spot, throw the hand and one or more fingers along the string into an extended position, then backwards into a folded position (see Diagram 22, p. 68).

142

5. *Combined Finger Throw and Arm Swing*
Play broken arpeggios, major and minor, such as the following, with one finger on one string:

These arpeggios should be played with each finger in turn (2, 4, 1, 3) on each string (D, E, G, A).

Then play major and minor scales, non-broken arpeggios and chromatic scales in the same way. The direction of the left-arm pivot and swing movements, as we saw in Lesson V (p. 119), depends on the direction of the bow. These should be exercised by starting all scales and arpeggios on both down- and up-bows. To ensure all keys are covered, I suggest following the cycle of major keys with their relative minors – C major, A minor; G major, E minor; etc. – one major and minor key each day. Practice of chromatic scales can be varied by including the exercise on p. 118 in which one finger remains on one spot while another slides chromatically up and down.

6. *Fingerfall and Trills*
Practise fingerfall on scales as described in Lesson V (pp. 114–15) and trills (see p. 122) with all possible combinations of the fingers on all four strings.

APPENDIX II

Care of the Violin and Bow

Never let resin or dust accumulate on the body of the violin. Wipe it often, but very lightly. Never touch any part of the varnished surface with your fingers; the body should be touched and held only at the chin-rest.

You may use softest old silk, Kleenex or cotton. Cotton is especially useful to clean under the fingerboard, tailpiece, chin-rest and bridge. Insert a thin piece of paper in the narrow spaces of the F holes to keep them free; treat the bridge in the same way. To polish your violin, use Hill's or some other reputable polish rarely and *very* sparingly, and see that no grease or oil is left to penetrate the wood. Keep fingerboard and strings clean with daily rubbings with purified benzine followed by alcohol, or with eau-de-cologne. The strings sound better and vibrate more freely when they are wiped clean of resin.

Every so often, insert a small handful of uncooked dry rice into the F holes. Shake it around inside the violin and then turn the instrument upside down: the grains of rice will fall out of the F holes, sometimes bringing a round ball of dust along with them.

The peg-box should be cleaned when we change strings, and the pegs checked for a tight fit. They can be rubbed at the circles of contact with a Hill stick which makes their motion both smooth and unslipping.

Use good strings. Personally, I prefer metal-wound gut A, D, and Gs, and aluminium-wound steel Es. But I recognise the practicality of the all-metal strings on very robust modern fiddles or violas. On old instruments the added tension strains the instrument and crushes the sound.

The bow stick must be absolutely straight. The bow should be rehaired as soon as hairs begin to break easily and as the first hairs to go are always on the outside of the bow, the remaining hairs will often twist and distort the stick. Clean the stick with alcohol, taking care that no moisture touches the bow hair.

Rehairing is a very precise and delicate job and should only be entrusted to qualified experts.